What Health Care Professionals Say About *Babywise II*

As an Asia and America-trained pediatrician, I know the principles of *Babywise II* work cross-culturally. Here is a resource that will help parents guide their babies with confidence and success through the three major transitions of the first year— feeding time, waketime and sleeptime. From experience with my two sons, my daughter and countless number of patients, I can enthusiastically recommend all the *Babywise* books as must-reads for competent parenting.

Saphry-May Liauw, M.D., M.S. (Pharm)
Jakarta, Indonesia

As a practicing pediatric neurologist, husband, and father, I fully endorse and highly recommend *Babywise II.* The principles found in this book are immensely practical and universally applicable. If the principles of structure and routine found in this resource were widely applied in the early months and years as they should be, I would see far fewer patients over the age of two with behavioral deficiencies and neurologic challenges. Virtually all of the books available on child development, behavior management and attention disorders fall far short when compared to the wisdom, practicality, and confidence offered in this one resource.

Robert P. Turner, M.D.
Richmond, Virginia

As a *Babywise* pediatrician, every newborn baby is a challenge and excitement to me, because I know I can help them with their moral behaviors as well as their physical well-being. *Babywise II* enables me to contribute to the structure and behavior of children, which is much needed in our society. This wonderful, practical, and effective book is an invaluable asset to my practice, since no other medical textbook strikes so deeply into the basic needs of life.

Peter Y. S. Kim, M.D.
Valencia, California

Finally, a parenting guide that is practical, makes sense and works! *Babywise II* provides today's parents with the up-to-date parenting strategies needed for a new millennium. As a pediatric professional, I enthusiastically recommend this book as a vital road map for the pre-toddler months.

Penn Laird, M.D.
Pediatric Cardiologist
Dallas, Texas

ON BECOMING

BABY WISE

BOOK TWO

Gary Ezzo, M.A., serves as the executive director of Growing Families International. He and his wife, Anne Marie, have spoken to millions of mothers, fathers, educators and medical clinicians through their best-selling books and weekend seminars. Their parenting concepts are now in twenty-seven languages. The Ezzos have two daughters, nine grandchildren, and reside in South Carolina.

Robert Bucknam, M.D., F.A.A.P. is the founder and director of Cornerstone Pediatrics in Louisville, Colorado, where he resides with his wife, Gayle. The Bucknams have four sons.

ON BECOMING BABY WISE

BOOK TWO

Parenting Your Five to Twelve-Month-Old
Through the Babyhood Transitions

PAN

This edition first published in India 2019 by Pan
an imprint of Pan Macmillan Publishing India Private Limited,
707, Kailash Building
26 K. G. Marg, New Delhi – 110 001
www.panmacmillan.co.in

Pan Macmillan, 20 New Wharf Road, London N1 9RR
Basingstoke and Oxford
Associated companies throughout the world
www.panmacmillan.com

ISBN 978-93-86215-90-1

On Becoming Babywise – Book Two:
Parenting Your Five to Twelve-Month-Old Through the Babyhood Transitions © 2012 Robert Bucknam and Gary Ezzo. Original English language edition published by Parent-Wise Solutions, Inc.

1 3 5 7 9 8 6 4 2

Typeset by Manmohan Kumar
Printed and bound in India by Gopsons Papers Ltd.

Dedicated To:
Robyn and Gary Vander Weide

Two points of light shining bright,
two friends walking close

Acknowledgements

We are grateful for the assistance of many co-workers from the past and the present, including, Tim and Patricia lentz, scott and Theresa Mcleod, David and cynthia Iglesias, Tiana Wendelburg, and sharon Augustson. They were all instrumental in the success of this book. We would also like to thank connie lamoureux who contributed the narrative on language development (Appendix A), and nancy Martin and sketch artist, Yvonne Wilber for their contributions on sign-language training. We are grateful for Tommye Gadol, Paige Hunter and Allicin Morimizu's recent editorial contributions, which we highly prize and greatly appreciate.

It takes talent to explain the neuroscience of a baby's brain and how parents can profoundly influence advanced forms of learning in their young children. The many references to an infant and toddler's developing brain come from the assistance of Dr. Robert Turner, a long-time friend and medical consultant. Dr. Turner's gifts of time and attention as a pediatric neurologist to the growing body of research and breakthroughs in neuroscience will benefit our readership for generations to come. We have another valuable resource in Dr. Alan Furness, a friend who provided recommendations for proper dental care of infants and toddlers. We also wish to extend our heartfelt thanks to rich and Julie Young, Greg and Tara Banks, and shawn and connie Wood for their multiple insights and practical suggestions that make *Babywise II* relevant to everyday living.

Contents

Preface

As a pediatrician, the healthy growth of children is the central concern of my practice. By definition, "healthy" means more than positive ear, nose, and throat examinations—it also implies emotional, physical, moral, and cognitive fitness. It includes giving a baby the best environment to grow, flourish and reach his or her full potential at each stage of development.

In our first book, *On Becoming Babywise*, we presented a number of self-evident truths relating to baby care, starting with the fact that infants thrive on order, routine and predictability. The benefits of these "nurturing virtues" are self-evident and easily confirmed by the amazing outcomes demonstrated by healthy growth, attentive waketimes, cognitive alertness and the formation of great naps and healthy nighttime sleep habits. However, such outcomes should not be viewed as trophies from the past, but stepping stones into the future. What has been gained thus far is only a down payment on what must be achieved during the next great transition—parenting your five to twelve-month-old.

This is truly an amazing and exciting phase of a baby's life, in part because babies achieve a level of alertness in which they begin to intentionally interact with people, places and things that make up their developing world. This is also a time of great cognitive expansion when Baby purposefully begins to make, literally, "baby decisions" from which learning patterns begin to take shape. Correspondingly, it is a time when Mom and Dad's actions and reactions profoundly impact those "baby decisions." This is why parenting in the second half of the first year moves out of the category of wonderfully-simple to challenging and complex.

How should a *Babywise* Mom and Dad approach the next growth transition? certainly not by abandoning that which has brought them so much success—their baby's routine. As a baby grows, his basic nutritional, sleep, cognitive and emotional needs do not change; but *how* those needs are met everyday will change. That is because babies never plateau but continue to grow, transitioning from one phase to another. As each new growth transition takes place, adjustments must be made to their feed-wake-sleep routine, in order to keep up with their changing and increasingly complex needs.

What do parents need to know about the changes and challenges just around the corner? In *Babywise II*, we connect all the dots between the passive world of infancy and the multiplicity of growth factors emerging during the second six months of life. The more parents understand the multifaceted babyhood transitions, the more confident they become in managing their baby's unfolding world. *Babywise II* is here to help with that challenge. Enjoy the journey.

Robert Bucknam, M.D.

Introduction

It's reality-check time! You're at least four months into your tour of parenting, and the complexities of child training are starting to multiply. While your baby is growing physically, his mind is adapting with ever-increasing awareness to new sights, sounds, sensations and relationships. He can now interact with his material universe with greater attentiveness. Watch out: big changes are coming to his world and yours!

Preserving the order and structure that brought security to your baby's day, peaceful sleep in your baby's nights and stability in your home are still key priorities, but now they must be viewed through a new developmental lens. For example, feeding time is more than a biological response initiated by a baby's sucking reflex. For the five-month-old, meal times become a complex and conscious interaction between child and parent, food and drink, preference and need, likes and dislikes, must do and won't do!

This is also when waketime behaviors and responses start to fall into the categories of safe or unsafe and right or wrong, and will either be encouraged or discouraged by how Mom and Dad react. Training to encourage right behavior and discourage wrong behavior will become the focus of Mom and Dad's attention over the next seven months. All those feeding, waking and sleep times provide numerous built-in opportunities for displaying parental wisdom, guidance and patience. *Babywise II* is here to help you in this crucial time.

The first edition of *Babywise II* was originally written for a U.S. audience and, as such, we used Imperial measurements, including ounces, pounds, and inches. However, with a growing international constituency, we understand the need to convert these figures to the Metric system of weights and measurements. On the next page we provided a simple metric weights and measurements conversion chart based on the measurements found in this book. Please note that the chart contains the "approximate" exchange for each unit of measurement referenced.

There are some matters of terminology we would like to address. In *Babywise*, the first book in this series, we introduced Parent-Directed Feeding *(PDF)*. In *Babywise II,* when we speak of the *PDF* baby, we are referring to an infant raised under the influence of the *Babywise* principles. The reader will also come across the phrase "babyhood transition months." This refers to the broad period of development between five and twelve months-of-age. In comparison, the term, "pretoddler" specifically refers to babies between nine to twelve months-of-age. When you read through each chapter, you will see that we predominantly used the masculine gender in our illustrations.

This was done for our convenience. The principles will, of course, work equally well with girls. Finally, the name of the child most often referred to in this book is "Baby."

Many rewarding experiences await you and your family as you enter this exciting phase of parenting. Enjoy each precious moment!

Gary Ezzo

Imperial-Metric Conversion Chart

(Approximate)

Dry Weight Oz to Grams	Conversion Lbs to Kg	Fluid Ounces Oz to Mls	Conversion Cups to Mls
½ – 15g	15 lbs –7kg	20 – 600 mls	1 – 250 mls
1 – 30g		24 – 700 mls	2 – 500 mls
1½ – 45g		32 – 950 mls	3 – 750 mls
2 – 60g			4 – 1 litre
3 – 85g			
3½ – 100g			
4 – 115g			
5 – 145g			
6 – 170g			
7 – 200g			
8 – 230g			

Section One

Your Baby from Five and Eight Months

Chapter One

Begin as You Mean to Go

Begin as you mean to go is more than a chapter title; it is a defining philosophy and a training slogan repeated throughout this book. We encourage parents to *begin as you mean to go* during the *babyhood transition months* (5–12 months), because this is a critical period of brain formation and adaptation. It is a time when parents are intentionally (or unintentionally) imprinting learning patterns that will stay with the child for many years to come. Since growth and development takes place in stages, with each new experience building upon the previous, it is imperative that the first learning patterns established be the right patterns—thus, *begin as you mean to go!*

Where should parents begin? In *On Becoming Babywise,* we put forth our foundational belief that babies, whose tender lives are guided by a predictable feed-wake-sleep routine, tend to function at optimal levels compared to babies who are not given the same advantage. That same belief guides this presentation. The feed-wake-sleep principles that governed the first five months will continue for the next seven months. However, in these later months, new growth variables come into play requiring a new level of parental insight and management to keep up with the changes.

Take food for example. As Baby approaches five or six months of age, rice cereal is usually introduced into his diet. On the surface, the step of offering cereal seems fairly straightforward. Mom takes a little powdered cereal, mixes with some breastmilk or formula, introduces a small spoon, and there you have it. Well, not quite! Mealtime is no longer a simple biological drive initiated by the sucking reflex. For the six-month-old baby, it becomes part of a very complex, conscious interaction between child and parent, food and drink, preference and need, likes and dislikes—all coupled with "must do" and "won't do!" Waketime is no longer a passive hour of an immobile infant observing the world from his blanket. Once mobility is achieved, Mom and Dad must continually chase after him just to keep him safe. What makes this phase exciting, and at the same time challenging, are the multifaceted growth changes taking place week by week.

One Phase, Two Adjustments

In "baby time" the amount of growth and development taking place between five and twelve months is staggering. The changes are so numerous and substantial that the phase is best divided into two smaller adjustment periods. There are the initial feeding adjustments starting around five or six months of age, which include the introduction of solid foods. As mealtimes become more involved, waketimes begin to extend. Longer waketimes require more planning and supervision. They also affect the number of naps required throughout the day.

The second adjustment phase starts around nine months of age, when the milestone of mobility requires more vigilance. Little crawling legs can now take Baby where his curious mind wants to go! This is also when he is sitting in his highchair, sometimes enjoying his food and sometimes playing with it, or deciding on his own that mealtime is over. He is now fully capable of demonstrating mild to fierce preferences toward food likes and dislikes, and will develop creative ways to voice his protest: from flipping his plate to blowing food out of his mouth! As his body grows, so does his mind, accompanied by an acquired understanding that his *actions* will generate *reactions* from Mom and Dad by the cute and not-so-cute things he does. That is when terms like *training* and *parental leadership* take on a whole new meaning and a greater sense of urgency!

To bring clarity to the specific changes about to take place with your baby, we designed *Babywise II* to parallel the two adjustment periods. In section One (chapters One through Five) we take up the feed-wake-sleep changes for months five to eight; in section Two (chapters six through Ten) we revisit the same activities, but for the nine to twelve-month-old.

As a parent you might wonder how much change can actually take place in three short months. We suggest you take plenty of photos of your five-month-old because at nine months, he will be a different child, possessing significant new abilities and deeper understanding of his world and everyone in it. By twelve months he emerges as a mobile pretoddler, driven by a desire to explore, discover and learn how to rule the world with a smile or a scream! Mom and Dad, welcome to babyhood transition months. Your life is about to change. What do you need to know?

FACTORS OF GROWTH

Throughout a baby's first year, two processes continue to dominate: growth and learning. These activities are interdependent, but are not interchangeable. Growth refers to the biological processes of life; learning refers to the mental processes, which include moral training and development. With both growth and learning, the building blocks are progressive. Each stage of development depends on the successful completion of the previous stage.

Every species, whether animal or human, follows a pattern of development peculiar to the species. Infants demonstrate two growth patterns: vertically, from the head down to the feet and horizontally from the central axis of the body toward the extremities. Descending vertical development means strength in physical structure and function come first to the child's head region, then to the child's trunk, and last to his legs and feet. Your baby first started to lift his head, bob it a little, and then let it fall back to the mattress. Next, he could hold his head upright as a result of his developing neck and chest muscles.

At the age of 20 weeks, he had control over the muscles of his eyes, head, and shoulders, but his trunk was still so limp that he had to be propped up or strapped in a chair to be able to maintain a sitting position. He made good use of his arms and hands in reaching and grasping before he could use his legs. He will eventually motor himself around by creeping, then crawling, and then walking, running, jumping, and skipping.

Horizontal development proceeds from simple to complex. In the prenatal state the head and trunk are well-developed before the limbs begin to grow. Gradually, the arms lengthen and then develop into the hands and fingers. Functionally, in the postnatal state, a baby can use his arms before his hands, and can use his hands as a unit, before he can control the movements of his fingers. He rakes his food toward his mouth first, before he can master the finer motor skill of the *pincer reflex*, which is the ability to pick up small objects with the thumb and index finger. Order is the operative word for biological maturation, because physical growth always occurs in an orderly, predictable manner.

FACTORS OF LEARNING

Biological maturation reflects changes in physical capabilities that result from genetic cues, but learning signifies changes that come from interacting with one's environment. For your baby, learning comes mainly from parental influence and instruction. Like adults, children interpret new experiences in relation to knowledge previously acquired. That means learning is progressive, and a child gains understanding when new information relates to his previous experiences. Routine and orderly transition at each stage of a child's development aid the connection between new information and your child's understanding. That is the meaning behind this chapter's title, *Begin As You Mean to Go.*

Allowing a child to progress in an orderly fashion in his new and expanding world greatly enhances his ability to learn. It is the gradual assimilation of many perceptions that gives rise to the formation of ideas. The child who can associate right meanings with new experiences is far more advanced in his understanding than the child who must associate a new meaning with an old situation that will ultimately need correction.

Since learning comes in progressive stages, child-training should take place in the same way, occurring in step with learning. For this reason, parents should provide their child with a learning environment that matches information with understanding. There are many influences on learning. Some of the more obvious ones include the child's temperament, the presence or absence of siblings, parental resolve, the purpose for training, the method of instruction and reinforcement. There are three general categories of learning: *basic skills*, *academic learning* and *moral development*. Let's consider each one.

Basic Skills

Not all behavior is moral in nature. Some actions are morally neutral, such as those related to basic skills. One of the most important and rapid areas of growth during early childhood is the development of motor skills. Learning to drink from a cup, use a spoon, and walk are skills mastered in stages. When your baby is introduced to finger foods, he begins by raking his food with his entire hand, then he lifts the food toward his mouth with his fist closed. As his coordination develops, he begins to use just his fingers and eventually his index finger and thumb, bringing food to his mouth with precision. In a few years, your toddler will throw a ball using his whole body. As his coordination develops, he will throw the ball using only his arm.

Skills, talents and giftedness are not the same thing. Skills, such as learning to use a spoon, to walk, to color within the lines, to ride a bike and to throw a ball, are basic to all human beings. Natural talents differ from skills in that they are discriminatory. All of us have talents, but not necessarily the same talents. Giftedness is a talent magnified. Many musicians are naturally talented, but Mozart was gifted.

Academic Learning

Academic learning is the accumulation of data and the ability to apply logic (reasoning skills) to a given situation. Academic learning, much like physical development, moves from general to specific and is progressive. We teach our children the alphabet, so they can learn to put letters together to form words and eventually read those words. They first learn to count 1, 2, 3, 4, 5, but it will be a while before they realize that those same numbers can also represent $12,345. Children first learn about trees in general, and then they begin to distinguish, for example, a pine tree from an oak. Eventually they may learn to identify the different varieties of pine trees. The connections in the brain that make those facts understandable to a child are not formed randomly, but through activity and purposeful training. Please keep that in mind!

Moral Development

At birth, a child has no functioning conscience, nor does a baby or pretoddler have the reasoning capacity to grasp right and wrong, good and evil. That does not mean parents should delay introducing required and acceptable behavior. For example, the fact that a child has no moral understanding of why food should not be intentionally dropped from his highchair does not mean parents should hold back instruction or fail to discourage the behavior.

With adults, beliefs precede actions, but with pretoddlers and toddlers, the opposite is true: actions precede beliefs. That is why parents should insist on right responses long before their children are capable of understanding why they are being required. Young children first learn how to act appropriately, and then they learn how to think appropriately. Just because a six-month-old baby is not capable of making moral decisions does not mean basic infrastructures for future moral behavior are not being established. They are!

The first step toward reasoning skills and comprehension is the development of healthy learning patterns and good habits. Structure in your baby's basic routine enhances those patterns, and the neuro-pathways in your baby's brain welcome them! When a child is at peace with his basic environment, his learning potential increases, and learning disorders diminish. Routine and order help bring about this desired result.

Routine and orderly advancement also encourage self-control. Self-control is a foundational virtue on which other virtues depend; such as kindness, gentleness, proper speech, controlling negative emotions, concentrating, focusing, sitting still and many other behaviors essential for learning. Who would have thought there were so many components of learning tied back to the babyhood transition months!

Chapter Two

Your Baby's Routine Past and Present

Why do most people read the first chapter of a book before the others? Most likely it is because of its location: it appears first. Why do authors design their chapters to present an unfolding sequence of ideas? They have the advantage of knowing how the *content* of one chapter fits into the broader *context* of the book. Content and context are inseparably linked as independent components of learning. A person can read the content of this chapter and walk away with some useful knowledge, but he or she will gain much more meaning after reading the entire book. Content without context is like possessing right knowledge but not understanding the big picture. You may have all the puzzle pieces, but without the box-cover picture, you are going to have a tough time trying to put the puzzle together.

Content and context are also vital concepts for parenting. With a baby in the home, you now have a family context that brings meaning to the content you learned before your baby was born. Now it is time to expand the content of what you are learning as parents, particularly about the rapid growth changes that will take place over the next six months.

MANAGING YOUR BABY'S ROUTINE

When researchers attempt to establish averages and expectations, they usually look at large population samples from which they statistically determine the boundaries of normal. From that data, they establish predictions and describe trends. That is what we have done with the expansive *Babywise* population.

As a *Babywise* mom and dad, you are already familiar with the three activities of a baby's day: feeding time, waketime, and naptime and with the general principle of *merging*. For example, most *Babywise* babies start life with nine feed-wake-sleep cycles in a 24-hour period. Over the first year, those nine cycles gradually begin to *merge*, one by one, until your baby's routine is comprised of just three feed-wake-sleep cycles in a 24-hour day: breakfast, lunch and dinner. Baby goes from four to five naps a day to two naps at the end of the first year and nine feedings are reduced to three feedings. How do those changes take place? What are the triggers? The three most urgent questions usually asked by eager *Babywise II* parents include:

1. What changes can we expect over the next six months?
2. When can we expect them?

3. What adjustments should we make in our routine to facilitate our baby's growth?

Uunfortunately, we cannot say, "Do this, this and this, and everything will fall into place." We know the average times when cycles begin to merge, but we cannot pinpoint the exact time they will take place with your baby. Fortunately, there are common-sense principles carried over from *Babywise* that can help any parent navigate the various feed-wake-sleep merges taking place during the babyhood transition phase. Let's see how they apply to *Babywise II*.

<u>One</u>: The principle of *capacity* and *ability*: A mother cannot arbitrarily decide to drop a feeding or adjust a naptime unless her baby has the physical capacity and ability to make the adjustment.

<u>Two</u>: The principle of *time variation*: While the length of each feed-wake-sleep cycle during the early weeks of life remains fairly consistent, eventually each cycle takes on its own unique features. For example, at four months of age, one feed-wake-sleep cycle might be as short as 2½ hours, while another might stretch to 3½ hours. At six months everything changes again. Some babies may have one waketime noticeably longer than the other waketimes during the day or one naptime that is shorter than the others. One cycle may be 3½ hours and another 4 or 4½ hours. The range depends on your baby's unique needs, the time of day and his age.

Three: The principle of *individuality* among children: All babies experience the same merge, but not at the same time. The merging of feed-wake-sleep cycles takes place according to your baby's biological schedule, which can be significantly different from your neighbor's baby down the street. For example, cory began sleeping 8 hours through the night at six weeks of age. Across town, his cousin Anna began sleeping 8 hours at night at ten weeks of age. That is a four-week difference. However, by 12 weeks, Anna began sleeping 12 hours a night, whereas cory never slept more than ten hours a night his entire first year. Although both babies had different outcomes, they fell within the normal range of expectation. They experienced the same two merges (dropping the middle-of-the-night and late-evening feedings, but at different times and according to their individual sleep needs).

Four: The *first–last* principle: the first and last feedings of the day are most strategic, no matter what is dropped, changed or merged in your baby's routine. Whether your baby is on a 3, 4 or 4½-hour routine, the entire day falls within those two fixed feeding times.

FROM PRINCIPLE TO PRACTICE

With the principles above serving as a guide, we now move to a short review of the seven major feed-wake-sleep merges of the first year. Afterward, we will look at specific details for the last four merges of your baby's first year.

(Merge One) Weeks 3–5: This is when most *Babywise* babies merged the two late-night feedings into one middle-of-the-night feeding. This reduced the 9 feed-wake-sleep cycles to 8 in a 24-hour period.

(Merge Two) Weeks 7–11: This is when most *Babywise* babies dropped their middle-of-the-night feeding and began sleeping 8 hours at night. That means 8 cycles are reduced to 7 cycles.

(Merge Three) Weeks 12–15: This is when most *Babywise* babies dropped their late-evening feeding and began sleeping 10–12 hours at night, reducing 7 cycles to 6.

(Merge Four) Weeks 16–24: This is when most *Babywise* babies begin to extend their morning waketime, reducing feed-wake-sleep cycles to 5. The introduction of solid foods naturally affects the various feed-wake-sleep cycles.

(Merge Five) Weeks 24–39: *Babywise* babies will begin replacing their third late-afternoon nap with a 30–45 minute catnap. Going from a full nap to a catnap does not eliminate a feed-wake-sleep cycle, but it moves your baby's routine in that direction.

(Merge Six) Weeks 28–40: This is when most *Babywise* babies drop their catnap. The new routine includes a morning and afternoon nap, along with three meals a day and a liquid feeding at bedtime.

(Merge Seven) Weeks 46–52: *Babywise* babies now transition to three meals a day, with an optional bedtime feeding for breast-feeding mothers. This basic routine might continue through 18 months of age, or until your baby drops his morning nap.

THE FINAL FOUR BABYHOOD MERGES

With the summary overview serving as a guide, we now take up the final four *Babywise II* merges. As we do, please keep in mind that, while all babies have similar nutritional and sleep needs, the timing of those needs can vary from one feed-wake-sleep cycle to another. One cycle might be 2½ hours, another 3 hours, and another 3½ hours. These ranges of time exist because some babies can tolerate a 3½ hour feed-wake-sleep cycle in the morning, while others can only handle a 3-hour routine. Regardless of the time variations within each cycle, cycles, they must all fit between the first and the last feedings of the day.

(Merge Four) Between Weeks 16–24: At four months of age, most babies still receive six feedings in a 24-hour period. At some point in time, between weeks 16 and 24, your baby's daytime needs will begin to change ushering in "Merge Four." six feedings a day will then be reduced to five feedings. What change does this merge bring? This is when most babies begin to extend their morning waketime.

To facilitate this merge, Mom must establish the two "fixed" feedings (first and last of the day) and readjust the other three feed-wake-sleep cycles, according to the baby's cues. This means there will be only one feed-wake-sleep cycle between breakfast and lunch (although lunch time usually is moved up at least a half hour). Adding to the mix is the possible introduction of solid foods. Solid foods will impact the length of each feed-wake-sleep cycle and will eventually trigger "Merge Five."

The sample time listed on the schedules are for illustration use only. We are using 7:00 a.m. as the first morning feed, but realize your baby may start at 6:00 a.m. or 8:00 a.m. or anytime in between. Personalize the times to fit your baby's needs.

Sample Schedule After Merge Four
(Weeks 16–24)

	Activities
1. Morning	
7:00 a.m.	1. Feeding
________	2. Waketime
________	3. Down for a nap
2. Late Morning	
________	1. Feeding
________	2. Waketime
________	3. Down for a nap
3. Early Afternoon	
________	1. Feeding
________	2. Waketime
________	3. Down for a nap
4. Late Afternoon	
________	1. Feeding, diaper change

________	2. Waketime*
________	3. Down for a nap

5. Mid-Evening

________	1. Early-evening waketime
8:00–8:30 p.m.	2. Liquid feeding, down for the night**

* Take note how the late-afternoon waketime activity extends into the early evening, concluding with the bedtime feeding. While there is no full nap-time between the two feedings in this feed-wake-sleep cycle, a baby may, on occasion, doze for 30–40 minutes, depending on when the late afternoon cycle began. This is referred to as a "catnap."

** Possible 11:00 p.m. "dream feed" for the breastfeeding Mom.

Note about "Dream Feeds": Mothers will commonly ask if there is a difference between the "late-evening feed" and the "dream feed" since they both fall around the same time at night. The answer is "Yes, there is a difference." The late-evening feeding provides the necessary nutrition Baby needs and is part of a baby's routine up through the first three months. The "dream feed" comes later, but it is not offered because the baby needs the calories, but to help the breastfeeding mom maintain her milk supply. Not all mothers need to offer a "dream feed," but the probability increases as Mom moves into her mid-30s.

<u>(Merge Five) Between Weeks 24 and 39</u>: Between five and seven months of age a *partial* feed-wake-sleep transition begins to take place, in part because of the introduction of solid foods, and in part due to the emergence of the "catnap". As noted

previously, the catnap is a transitional nap, shorter in length but still necessary. It happens when a baby no longer needs the additional sleep of a full afternoon nap, but he is not quite ready to go without a short rest. Catnaps usually occur in the very late afternoon, often around dinnertime.

When do *Babywise* babies drop their third "full" nap and move to a catnap? It can happen anytime between 24–39 weeks. This large span of time represents a huge variation among babies, yet the span of weeks falls within the "normal" range of predictable behavior. It is just a unique fact of individuality that some babies will drop the "full nap" and replace it with a catnap within a month's time, while other babies appear stuck in *Merge Four*, and continue their three naps a day well into the seventh month. Once your baby drops his third "full" nap, his daytime feed-wake-sleep cycles can range between 3½ to 4 hours or possibly, for some babies, 4½ hours each day. This will depend on the time of day and your baby's unique needs.

Sample Schedule After Merge Five
(24–39 Weeks with *Catnap*)

	Activities
1. Morning	
7:00 a.m.	1. Feeding
________	2. Waketime
________	3. Down for a nap
2. Late Morning	
________	1. Feeding

________	2. Waketime
________	3. Down for a nap

3. Mid-afternoon

________	1. Feeding
________	2. Waketime
________	3. Down for catnap*

4. Late Afternoon/Dinner Time

________	1. Feeding
________	2. Waketime

5. Early Evening

________	1. Early-evening waketime
8:00–8:30 p.m.	2. Liquid Feeding; Down for the night

* This is usually around dinnertime, between 5:00 p.m. and 6:00 p.m.

<u>(Merge Six) Between Weeks 28 and 40</u>: Between weeks 28–40, most *Babywise* babies drop their catnaps reducing the five feed-wake-sleep cycles to four, which include breakfast, lunch, dinner and a liquid feeding at bedtime. Again, please notice the span of weeks separating Merge Five and six. We previously mentioned the nighttime sleep trends for cory and Anna. When it came to dropping his catnap, cory did so at 29 weeks of age and transitioned beautifully into to "Merge seven." Meanwhile, across town, his cousin Anna hung on to her catnap until 39 weeks. Here again is an example of two babies responding to their individual sleep needs, but falling within the "normal" range for dropping their catnaps. Your new schedule will look something like this:

Sample Schedule After Merge Six (28–40 Weeks *no Catnap*)

	Activities
1. Breakfast	
7:00–8:00 a.m.	1. Feeding
________	2. Waketime
________	3. Down for a nap
2. Midday	
________	1. Feeding
________	2. Waketime
________	3. Down for a nap
3. Late Afternoon	
________	1. Feeding*
________	2. Waketime
________	3. Dinner time with family**
________	4. early evening waketime
4. Bedtime	
8:00 p.m.	1. liquid feeding, down for the night***

* Baby will receive his cereal, vegetables, and/or fruits at this feeding.

** Baby joins family mealtime with light finger foods. (This is more of a snack than a full meal.)

*** Initially, with only two naps a day, there may be occasions when an earlier bedtime might be needed.

<u>(Merge Seven) Between Weeks 46 and 52</u>: The only adjustment made with this merge is dropping the fourth liquid feeding

right before bedtime. You might offer a cup of formula, breastmilk, or water, but a bottle of milk is not necessary. Congratulations! You have come a long way since the early weeks and the original nine feed-wake-sleep cycles.

Sample Schedule After Merge Seven
(46–52 Weeks)

	Activities
1. Breakfast	
7:00 a.m.	1. Feeding
________	2. Waketime
________	3. Down for a nap
2. Midday	
________	1. Feeding
________	2. Waketime
________	3. Down for nap
3. Late Afternoon	
4:00–4:30 p.m.	1. Snack after nap
________	2. Waketime
________	3. Dinner time with family
________	4. early evening waketime
4. Bedtime	
8:00 p.m.	1. Down for the night

SUMMARY

This last merge will continue to serve Baby and the rest of the family up through 18 months of age. Although some *Babywise* babies might drop their morning naps as early 15 months or as late as 24 months, your baby will give you all the signs, when it is the right time for him.

By now, as a Dad and Mom you have become masters at working your baby's routine. All needs are being met according to his timetable of developing needs, and your little person is responding beautifully. The secret for success is still in the term, "Parent-directed." As a mom and dad, you will decide what is best for your baby and when the proper adjustments should be made. This decision will not be based on the experience of others, but it will be based on the unique needs of your baby.

Chapter Three

Common Mid-Transition Questions

Sometimes it is difficult to move forward without first taking a few steps back. As parents move from the early days of infancy toward the mid-year mark, subtle growth shifts begin to influence the various feed-wake-sleep cycles during the day. These small but significant changes in growth usually spawn a number of questions that are peculiar to the four and five month "mid-transition" phase of development. While the questions are unique to each baby, they tend to fall into some predictable sequence.

We trust the following question and answer interchange will fall somewhere between helpful and informative, encouraging and corrective. The questions represent the most common inquiries received from our *Babywise* community relating to this narrow mid-transition phase.

Question One: realizing that some feedings will come sooner than others, how much flexibility can a four-month-old handle in his routine? can some cycles be three hours and other cycles four hours, or should I work to keep everything the same?

Answer: regardless of your child's age, a basic routine offers Mom and Baby plenty of flexibility with time increments. This becomes more evident as Baby grows. While the length of each feed-wake-sleep cycle during the early weeks of life remains fairly consistent, eventually over time, each cycle will have its own unique features. For example, at four months of age, one feed-wake-sleep cycle might be as short as 2½ hours, while another cycle may stretch to 3½ hours. At six months, everything changes again. Some babies have a longer waketime or possibly shorter naptime impacting a particular cycle. This is why one cycle may be 3½ hours, another cycle 4 hours (or possibly 4½ hours). The range of variation depends on your baby's unique needs, time of day, and his age. Where Mom has less flexibility is with the first and last feedings of the day. Those should remain fairly consistent.

Question Two: We worked with our three-month-old son to drop his late evening feeding by backing it up from 11:00 p.m. to 10:30 p.m., and then to 10:15 p.m. But now our son is waking at 5:00 in the morning, and his routine morning feeding is around 7:00 a.m. should we go back to the 11:00 p.m. feeding, or do something different in the morning?

Answer: While transitioning from 8 hours of nighttime sleep to 9 or 10 hours, it is not uncommon for babies to wake earlier than their normal morning feed. But what can or should Mom do about it? There are three workable options tied to this waking early challenge. First, Mom might wait 10 to 15 minutes to make sure her son is truly awake, because he might be passing through an "active" sleep state, moving to deeper sleep. Second (and the most commonly employed strategy), Mom might feed him at 5:00 a.m. and put him back down for more sleep. She can then start his day when he wakes. For example, if he wakes at 8:00 a.m., make that time be the new "first feeding," and then adjust the rest of the baby's day accordingly. Third, offer Baby a feeding at 5:00 a.m., treating it as the first feeding of the day. In that situation you would adjust the rest of the baby's day schedule, and Mom's as well.

Question Three: My goal is to breastfeed for a year. How can I keep up my milk supply, if my baby is sleeping 12 hours at night?

Answer: As a baby extends his nighttime sleep to 10 hours, Mom must stay mindful of her milk production. Allowing a baby to sleep longer than 10 hours at night may not provide enough feedings in a 24-hour period for sufficient stimulation. Therefore, if you are breastfeeding, maintain the 10:00 p.m. or 11:00 p.m. "dream feed." Many moms report their babies will nurse without waking, but yet, still take a good feeding.

Question Four: lately, my baby is waking halfway through his naps. I know he is not fully rested. What is going on here, and what should I do when this happens?

Answer: In chapter seven of *Babywise*, we offered a variety of reasons why a baby might periodically or consistently wake early out of a sound nap. Topping the list of many possibilities are two that relate to waketimes. Here is the connection. Some waketimes are too short, and some may be too long or over-stimulating. For example, your baby might be doing great during his waketime; but as he grows, waketimes are not being extended because Mom loves the schedule Baby is on right now. However, with growth comes necessity for adjustment in the amount of sleep needed. In most cases this will mean some adjustments to Baby's naptime, which will have an impact on the length of his waketimes. In the case above, the baby is most likely waking early because he is not sufficiently tired. The fix is easy—extend his waketime.

On the other hand, some waketimes may be sufficient in length but over-stimulating, or the waketime activity might be fine, but the waketime is too long. Both the over-tired and the over-stimulated baby become hyper-alert—fighting off sleep by waking early and crying.

Mom should evaluate all the activities of her day. Are you excessively busy? Are there too many visitors dropping by who have an irresistible urge to hug, hold, play with or entertain your baby? Are you spending too much time away from home?

This can be a source of over-stimulation, especially when baby is going along for the ride. The coming and going from here and there, the new sights and sounds, along with the absence of predictability, all work against good naps.

Catnaps in a car seat will sometimes come in handy, but they should never be considered a substitute for full naps in the crib, especially during the first year.

Question Five: We recently visited relatives, and our daughter was held and entertained the entire two weeks. Now at home, everything is out of whack. Is there an easy way to get her back on her routine?

Answer: Whether it is a weekend away or a short vacation, there are some adjustments to make when Mom, Dad and Baby return home. As a general rule, it may take upwards to 40% of the time away, that is needed to get your baby back on his "normal" routine. If you are away from home for two weeks, it may take three to five days before everything returns to normal. Four weeks away may take up to ten days before everything is back to normal with your baby. Speaking of "normal," try to resume your normal routine as soon as possible because that is where familiarity lies. Your baby's room, crib, highchair, living room sounds and favorite toys are all part of what makes up "normal" in her life.

Question six: My baby is four months old. Is it too early to introduce rice cereal?

Answer: Babies are highly individual when it comes to showing a readiness for solid foods. One baby might show signs at four months, while another shows no signs of readiness until six months. As a general rule, babies usually start between four and six months of age, although some research suggests that holding off solids to five or six months may decrease the possibility of food allergies. Please note, the research is not suggesting that by offering solids at four months you will create food allergies, but rather that some babies have an underdeveloped ability to digest solid foods, which is reflected by food allergies.

The American Academy of Pediatrics (AAP) leans toward six months before starting solids, but most grandmothers will tell you anytime between four and six months is appropriate, if your baby shows all the signs. Your baby's pediatrician or family practitioner will guide you based on your child's unique nutritional needs. (The developmental "signs" that signal your baby is ready for solid foods are found in the next chapter.)

Question seven: Our four-month-old is on a great schedule. Unfortunately, I have to go back to work. What are the main challenges that I might face as a Mom, when it comes to my need to balance my employment life with my role as a wife and mother?

Answer: Throughout the journey of motherhood, there may be seasons when financial need or a professional commitment require employment outside the home. For these moms, whether working full or part-time, the burden of parenting will multiply, as well as the emotional stress and physical fatigue that comes from trying to balance employment, marriage and parenting. We understand the challenges that employment can bring. If this section speaks to you, please know that there are some strategies that can help relieve some of the tension and minimize fatigue. Here are a few thoughts:

1. Returning back to work for the new mom is never easy. It can create emotional stress in the form of doubt, guilt or questions about her womanhood. She might wonder, as a wife, "Am I neglecting my husband?" As a mother, "Am I neglecting or abandoning my baby?" Or as a woman, "Am I neglecting my home?" These are legitimate feelings and concerns. However, mothers are not alone when it comes to doubt, fear and guilt. There are challenges husbands wrestle with, including feelings of not being a good provider for their families or protectors of their wives. While these are different concerns, they are legitimate feelings that Mom and Dad should openly and honestly talk through.

2. When speaking to a day-care provider, whether it is an individual sitter or in an institutional setting, find out what their "normal" day looks like. What type of routine do they follow, and what is the child-to-worker ratio? The key to your baby's routine is the feed-wake-sleep cycle. How close does the day care come to that basic flow? You may find the day care's routine is not that much different than yours.

3. Cooperative leadership is part of the parenting equation that brings Dad into the picture. He should be a willing partner, sharing in the mechanics of home life; doing laundry or taking on more kitchen duties, either by preparing a meal or cleaning up afterwards. Basically, he does whatever it takes to help relieve pressure from Mom. There may be times when "take out" food is the easiest thing to do and more likely to be better tasting than a hastily-prepared meal.

4. Accept the fact that when both parents are employed outside the home, it may mean sacrificing some time with friends or less time with hobbies; the house may not be immaculate, and parenting goals will not be achieved quite as fast as your stay-at-home friends. But they will be achieved in time, as long as both parents are committed to each other and the basic priorities of their parenting.

5. Reprioritize some of the evening responsibilities so Mom can get to bed earlier. Some activities can be moved to another time slot during the day. For example, use your lunch hour instead of the evening hours to run errands, pay bills, return phone calls, and send personal correspondence.

6. Allows stay mindful of your health. Not eating properly or drinking enough fluids also contribute to fatigue. Certain medications can make moms over-tired as well. As a mom pay particular attention to the labels and warnings on any over-the-counter medications. Some items, such as antihistamines, pain

relievers, or any stimulants can suppress sleep, and, therefore, add to the feeling of being fatigued.

A Word to the Single Mom

The working single mom will, of course, experience more pressure on her home life and parenting. Nonetheless, many of the principles above apply to her situation. Since she is parenting and managing a home without a spouse, she should let other people know of her needs. Seeking outside help from her local community services is one way. Local schools or youth groups might have a list of teens available to do lawn work or help around the house as a service project. We know from experience that when these little ideas mentioned above begin to merge together, they tend to create some big relief for the fatigued and stressed working mom, especially when parenting alone.

Chapter Four

Introducing Solid Foods

Parents are naturally concerned about the nutritional health of their babies, and for good reason. Infants have unique caloric needs, and between four to six months of age, those needs become more complex, requiring additional food sources. For most babies, this is when the introduction of solid foods begin.

Any consideration of a baby's diet should give special attention to what a child eats, as well as how many calories he eats. This chapter provides a general overview of both factors, starting with the various food groups that will soon become part of your baby's diet. We will then take the reader through the step-by-step process of introducing each food group into a baby's diet, according to their time table of needs.

THE FIVE BABY-FOOD GROUPS

If the modern mom only had to deal with a basic selection of cereals, vegetables and fruits, the task of introducing solid foods would be fairly easy. The challenge comes with the ever-increasing assortment of food combinations offered by baby-food manufactures. On store shelves today, you will find cereals mixed with fruits, vegetables in cereals, and fruits combined with vegetables. Multiply the number of vegetables with the number of fruits, and the final figure explains why baby food takes up half an aisle at the grocery store. The good news is that babies do not need to sample every food variety, but they do need the basic nutrition derived from the various food groups.

One thing mothers soon learn is that babies have no food or flavor expectations until they are created by the foods served. For that reason, we recommend keeping each food group separate until all have been introduced. After that, feel free to explore the various cereal/fruit or fruit/vegetable combinations.

The five food groups include cereals, vegetables, fruits, meats and juices. Cereals, vegetables and fruits are usually introduced when Baby is between six and eight months of age, but meats can be held off until ten months of age or older. Juices can be delayed until Baby's first birthday or longer since they have limited nutritional value.

Cereals: While there are three cereal options, pediatricians usually recommend rice cereal first because it causes the least amount of allergic reaction for Baby. Once rice cereal has been introduced successfully, you may want to consider introducing the other two options, oat and barley cereal.

Vegetables: After the introduction of cereals the next food source are vegetables. Vegetables should be introduced according to color categories, the most common being the yellow and green varieties. Most moms start with the yellow vegetables, such as squash, sweet potatoes and carrots, then move to the green vegetables, including peas and green beans. (In our next chapter we explain why it is best to introduce vegetables according to their color groups, and how long it will take.)

Fruits: After successfully introducing yellow and green vegetables, fruits are the next entree. While fruits make up an important nutritional component in a baby's diet, they are not as important as cereal and vegetables. As a mom, you can hold off introducing fruits until after seven to eight months of age.

Meats: Meats are protein-rich and include chicken, turkey, beef and ham. Since babies usually receive plenty of protein from breastmilk or formula, meats can be held off until ten months of age or older.

Juices: After the introduction of meats come the "fun foods," the juices. However, since juices do not offer any additional nutritional value that a baby is not already receiving from fruits, they can be held off until after Baby's first birthday.

INTRODUCING THE "SIPPY" CUP

While you may hold off introducing juices, we do not suggest delaying the introduction of the sippy cup. The American

Academy of Pediatrics suggests that children move completely to a "sippy cup" by their first birthday. This speaks not only to a child's ability to handle a cup, but also to Mom and Dad's need to be proactively training with a cup.

Sippy cups come in an assortment of colors, shapes, sizes and styles. As it relates to the baby, it should be one that is easy to hold; as it relates to Mom, it should be one with a "no drip/ no spill" feature. Sippy cups with straws attached have benefits for baby and Mom. When comparing the two styles, a regular sippy cup requires three steps: *tilt*, *sip*, and *swallow.* A sippy cup with a straw requires two steps, *sip* and *swallow*.

The sippy cup with a straw also has a "go anywhere" advantage. If out to a restaurant, visiting a friend, or on a long trip, all Mom needs to do is use a cup and a straw to be in her child's familiarity zone. If her baby, however, is only familiar with a regular sippy cup (no straw), Mom might find him doing more tilting and spilling instead of sipping and swallowing.

Introducing the sippy cup as early as six months of age has a number of benefits, one being convenience: nothing has to be prepared. Fill with water, refrigerated formula, or breastmilk, and take it on an outing or offer it after Baby wakes from his afternoon nap. Thinking futuristically for the nursing mother, at a year of age Baby can be weaned directly to a cup, rather than weaned to an unfamiliar bottle and then to the cup. (You will read about the weaning process in section Two.)

From this basic introduction of solid foods we now move to the specific step-by-step process of introducing each of the food groups. As we do, keep in mind that feeding your baby solid foods is not just a "Mom" thing. There is plenty of room for Dad's involvement—and plenty of need for it!

A Word to Dad

In the sphere of family life, no father has the luxury of just one job. When leaving his place of employment, he returns to the most important vocation of life: being a husband and father. Every dad knows what it is like to walk through the door after a busy day at work, only to discover he is needed even more at home.

Some would say this is just part of a father's obligation or his reasonable duty to help around the house. We never felt that way. It is not just a matter of providing a helping hand now and then, or a convenient way to interact with a son or daughter during a meal, but a way to take advantage of the simple, the pure and the good things of life. Choosing the joy associated with being in the presence of your children is not an obligation, but a lifestyle of choice that has broader community impact. Even something as basic as feeding a baby has its rewards of pleasure and satisfaction, and contributes to a father's public identity.

The positive consequence of a man having the right priorities in the home is a healthy sense of respect and appreciation that the community reflects back to him. Men who are known for being caring and loving husbands and involved fathers reflect to their community of peers confidence, trustworthiness, and believability. These are the silent virtues that ultimately define him as a man and leader within the community. There is more reward contained in those ordinary moments of family time than anything a day job can offer.

INTRODUCING SOLID FOODS STEP BY STEP

At a quick glance, the process of adding solid foods to a baby's diet seems relatively simple, if you are only looking at the mechanics involved: a small spoon, pureed food and a hungry baby. However, as previously noted, there is more going on at mealtime than just filling up a little tummy. Mom and Dad will now begin to experience some resistance and challenge to their loving and tender leadership. That is partly due to the change in menu. For the first five to six months of life following birth, most babies only have one entrée to choose from—milk! With the introduction of solid foods, something extraordinary begins to take place. Your baby is not simply being introduced to new foods, but to a world of *choice,* where he begins to acquire likes, dislikes, preferences and a blossoming willpower to battle Mom and Dad over what should and should not be on today's menu.

As choices become part of a baby's life, an entirely new realm of training opportunities becomes part of Mom and Dad's lives. For example, what happens when your baby shows preferences for one food over another, or suddenly and arbitrarily decides he no longer enjoys the taste of a particular food? What will you do? What about his little hands? Will they be free to explore his food or mix it with his hair? What happens when he discovers the joy of dropping food on the floor because he has learned that the dog will respond? How will you respond? Those are only a few of the common challenges that as a parent you will be confronted with routinely, and you must decide how you are going to handle them.

THE BASICS

One would think that eating comes as naturally as breathing, but it doesn't. Eating solid food requires new skills and plenty of adaptation. For example, your baby has never had a spoon repeatedly placed in his mouth before—let alone a spoon with food on it! This new action and accompanying sensations take a little time to get use to. In fact, your baby will initially push out with his tongue the little bit of food you put into his mouth. This predictable response is called *tongue thrusting* and should not be interpreted that he does not like his food, but simply he does not yet know what to do with it. He has never experienced swallowing solid food, which is different from gulping and swallowing milk. Realizing that solid foods differ in both taste and texture from breastmilk or formula also helps in understanding why there may be an initial resistance to a new food source being placed in Baby's mouth. However, this particular challenge will not last long, because babies are hard-wired to adapt to changes that accompany their growth.

Signs of Readiness

As mentioned previously, solid foods should be introduced only after a baby can hold his head up and is able to sit up (with support). Typically, this corresponds to the time he is able to lift his head off a blanket and sustain that position. Until those skills are well established, a baby should receive his daily nourishment through breastmilk or formula.

Other indicators of readiness include the doubling of your baby's birth weight (or weighing close to 15 pounds), and showing signs of hunger, even though he is receiving 32 oz. of formula a day, or six full breastfeeds in a 24-hour period. Further, any abnormal waking at night between five and six months of age, or waking early during naps are likely indicators that your baby's needs more nutrition during the day.

The Five Food Stages

Because a baby's calorie needs change with growth, baby-food manufacturers categorize food servings into stages. Each stage represents another level including food mixture, nutritional complexity and amounts per serving. You will also note these changes by the three different-size jars or containers available in stores (small for stage One, medium for stage Two and large for stage Three). Here is a summary of the Five stages:

Stage One: (4 to 6 months) single-grain cereal and single ingredient baby foods.

Stage Two: (6 to 7 months) single-ingredient servings or a combination of vegetables and fruits for added flavor and variety.

Stage Three: (8 to 12 months) A new range of textures, slightly coarser than pureed foods, packaged in larger containers for growing appetites. (At this age the AAP recommends a baby receive between 750 to 900 calories each day with 400 to 500 coming from breastmilk or formula.)

Stage Four: (12 to 15 months) Regular family meals supplemented with some baby food.

Stage Five: (15 months and up) Regular family meals, no baby food supplement necessary.

Checking for Allergic Reactions

Between four and seven months of age, a baby's intestinal lining goes through a growth process referred to as *"gut closure."* This is when the intestinal lining becomes more discriminating in what it allows to pass through. Breastfed babies tend to experience closure before formula-fed babies. This fact may explain why breastfed babies can actually handle the introduction of solid foods without allergic reaction before formula-fed babies.

A basic rule of introducing solids is to begin with one item at a time, waiting three to five days before introducing another new food type to see if your baby develops an allergic reaction. Such sequential introduction of food items allows you to monitor your baby's reaction so adjustments can be made if needed. For example, your baby might do fine with yellow squash, but have a reaction to peas. Tummy discomfort, diarrhea, or even rashes are common symptoms of food allergies, and all can affect naps and nighttime sleep. Vomiting, while rare, is a more serious indicator that baby is having a reaction. Never introduce multiple food types at the same time. If you do, you will not know which food caused the reaction, if one occurs.

When introducing cereal into a baby's diet, we recommend that mothers begin with the morning meal. If a baby does have an intestinal reaction, it will be noticed and should pass by the end of the day. However, if Mom introduces a new food at noon or at dinner, then she runs the risk of pushing any potential reaction to the middle of the night, when the causes of the sleep disturbances are more difficult to discern. Nighttime parenting, in such cases, is hard on everyone.

Finally, before starting solids, there is some wisdom in checking with immediate and extended family members to find out if there is a history of food allergies. Knowing whether allergies run in the family gives you a big advantage: If there is a history on either side, a higher probability exists that your little one will be challenged by food allergies. If it happens, at least you are not caught off guard.

GETTING STARTED

The introduction of solid foods does not mean the suspension of liquid feedings, as the calories gained from breastmilk or formula are still of prime importance. However, your baby is reaching a growth point where neither solid foods nor liquid feedings alone are nutritionally sufficient. Both are required, because your baby's body needs additional amounts of trace elements that cannot be found sufficiently in mother's milk or formula alone.

Iron and zinc, for example, are essential for your baby's physical growth and brain development, and both are contained in infant cereal, along with vitamins c and D. Babies need vitamin c to aid their immune system and process iron; vitamin D helps them develop strong bones and teeth. While breastmilk is the perfect initial food for your baby, breastfeeding mothers should be taking vitamin D supplements, especially if they continue to breastfeed after five months. Continuing with prenatal vitamins helps meet this nutritional requirement. (Bottle-fed babies receive their daily requirements of vitamin D from formula.)

Another point of encouragement for first-time Moms is to be patient with the process of introducing solid foods. Learning to swallow solids from a spoon is a new skill. The first few feedings will be a little messy, until your baby adapts, usually in one to three days. Do not be overly alarmed if it appears your baby is losing interest in eating before you think he should. You will discover over the next several months that your baby, like you, will not be equally hungry at each meal. Signs that he is full include: turning his head away from the spoon, thrusting food out of his mouth, or beginning to cry. You can complete the meal by breastfeeding or offering a bottle of formula, or just move to the next waketime activity.

Introducing Cereal

The first serving utensil is a spoon, and whether it has a rubber tip or metal surface does not really matter because your baby does not know the difference. He has never compared the two and formed an opinion! It has been suggested that bottle-fed infants might show a small preference for plastic-tip spoons because they are used to a latex or rubber nipple on the bottle. We do not know if that is a fact, but regardless, all babies adjust to whatever Mom offers. As every mother discovers, her baby will be more interested with the food on the spoon than the spoon itself.

As we previously stated, there are three cereal food sources that can and should become part of a baby's diet: rice, oat and barley. Rice cereal is the most common, because it causes the least amount of allergic reactions. The downside of rice cereal is a potential constipation problem. This is something to monitor, and if it is routinely occurring, it should be brought to the attention of your baby's pediatrician. If your pediatrician determines that rice cereal is not best for your baby, oat and barley cereals are two excellent substitutes.

We encourage Moms to introduce all three cereals over the course of a few months. The only grain to avoid initially is wheat cereal because it is a common allergen. New studies suggest that wheat cereal can be introduced as early as nine months, but our recommendation is to wait until after Baby's first birthday. There are no nutritional advantages gained by using wheat cereal that the other three cereals are not already providing.

HOW TO BEGIN?

Your cereal adventure begins on Day One.

Day One: start by mixing 1 tablespoon of rice cereal with 4 tablespoons of breastmilk, formula or water. (The texture after mixing should be similar to cream of Wheat.® It should not be overly-thick like a paste, or so watery that it drips off a spoon.) Although you will be increasing the amounts of cereal and liquid in the future, keep the consistency the same. Breakfast is the best meal to begin introducing cereal.

Day Two: Mix 2 tablespoons of rice cereal with liquid and offer at breakfast.

Days Three and Four: Increase the mixture to 3 tablespoons on the third day and 4 tablespoons on the fourth day. Maintain consistency by gradually increasing the amount of liquid. Cereal can now be offered at breakfast and lunch.

Day Five: If there are no allergic reactions by the end of Day Four, start offering cereal 3 times a day, using approximately 1/4 cup per meal.

Once beyond the first week, begin offering your baby solids at the normal feeding times. For example, if you have been breast or bottle feeding at 7:00 a.m. (breakfast), 11:00 a.m. (lunch), 3:00 p.m. (dinner), and 7:00 p.m., then solids should accompany at least the three major meals. Eventually baby's feeding times will align themselves with that of the family. Since cereal is an excellent source of iron, continue at least one serving per day up through the first year.

Combining Breastfeeding and Solids

A breastfeeding mom must stay mindful of protecting her milk supply. Continue with at least five nursing periods each day, three of which will be supplemented with solid foods: at breakfast, lunch and dinner. The two times a day when your baby is receiving just breastmilk are right after the afternoon naps and just before bedtime.

One caution when combining breastfeeding with solid foods: *Do not offer solid foods first and then try to nurse.* As your baby becomes more efficient at consuming solid food, he will be less interested in nursing. Less stimulation leads to a drastic reduction in Mom's ability to produce sufficient milk for the day. Instead, nurse *first* from both sides and then offer the solids.

If you are bottle feeding, offer 2 ounces, then solids, followed by the remaining amount of formula. Once you start adding solids to your baby's diet, his daily intake of milk should gradually decrease from 32 ounces a day to 24 ounces. After your baby is established on all solid foods, he should receive at least 20 ounces of formula per day alongside a varied diet until he is a year old. (Pediatricians normally do not advise moving from formula to cow's milk until after Baby's first birthday.)

Be careful not to offer solid foods, nurse 2 hours later and offer more solids 2 hours after that. You do not want to unwittingly train your child to snack and disrupt well-established patterns of healthy naps and nighttime sleep.

Introducing Vegetables

Once your baby is receiving three cereal portions a day, he is ready for vegetables. Start with yellow vegetables (squash or carrots) at the first meal of the day. Watch for any allergic reaction over the next three to four days before introducing green vegetables (peas or beans). Over time, expand the choices of primary vegetables to those most familiar to your family.

Serving Portions

Reading the labels on baby-food jars and cereal boxes is a good habit to get into because there you will find the ingredient list, suggested portion size and storage instructions. Stage one baby-food jars contain 2½ ounces of food. Stage two jars contain 3½ ounces. Each time you introduce another food group (vegetables, fruits or meats), start with half a jar or less for a few days, watching for excessive fussiness, rashes, runny nose, diarrhea or watery eyes.

By days four and five, increase the vegetables to one small jar twice a day, usually at lunch and dinner. Please think long-term by gradually offering your baby a variety of food tastes. This will decrease the probability of developing a picky or finicky eater. Such foward thinking is all part of *begin as you mean to go*.

At Stage two (six to seven months), move to the larger baby-food jars and serve approximately 3 ounces at least twice a day (one jar at lunch and one at dinner). You can continue this through the eighth month, or until you begin offering home-prepared vegetables.

When you do introduce vegetables, start looking for changes in your baby's skin color. Some babies enjoy squash and carrots so much that parents make them the vegetable of choice. However, too many yellow vegetables in a baby's diet can turn the skin tone slightly orange. This harmless condition is known as *carotenemia* because of the carotene levels in yellow vegetables. If you notice this condition, just reduce the amount of yellow vegetables in your baby's diet.

INTRODUCING FRUITS

Because fruits are a pleasure food and naturally more enjoyable than vegetables, they should be introduced with a healthy dose of wisdom. Mom must be careful not to encourage a preference of fruits over vegetables by serving fruits first. She can stay mindful of this by viewing fruits as a dessert rather than part of the main course, keeping cereals and vegetables first and fruit servings last.

Which Fruit First?

Most moms begin with applesauce, pears, peaches and bananas. As with all new foods, start at breakfast, and eventually move Baby's fruit serving to twice a day, which in time can be lunch and dinner (although fruits can also be a regular part of breakfast.)

How Much Fruit at Each Serving?

5–6 months: 1½ to 2 oz. twice a day
7 months: 3 to 4 oz. twice a day
8 months: 4 to 6 oz. twice a day
9–12 months: Mashed or small pieces of fresh fruit.

Not all fruits or similar foods are safe or digestible for babies. Avoid serving the following until after your baby's first birthday or as recommended by your baby's pediatrician:

Honey*	Sweeteners
Whole grapes	Large pieces of Fruit
Fruits with skin on it	Fruits with Seeds
Blackberries	Raspberries
Strawberries	Citrus Juices*

* Do not feed honey, corn syrup and other types of sweeteners to a baby under a year of age. They can be fatal to a baby because of the microorganisms they can harbor. Citrus has a high acidity rates that create tummy discomfort in babies under a year. If you have any hesitation or questions regarding a particular food source, check with your baby's pediatrician.

Eventually your baby's solid-food menu will look as simple as this:

Breakfast: Cereal and fruits
Lunch: Vegetables and fruits
Dinner: Cereal, vegetables, and fruits

INTRODUCING MEATS

The protein-food group is necessary to help build muscle and strengthen the immune system. Members of this group include turkey, chicken and varieties of beef. Since your baby is receiving highly digestible protein from breastmilk or formula, there is no urgency to add meats into your baby's diet until stage three (8–12 months) or longer. A 2½-ounce serving a day is sufficient to meet your baby's protein needs. Like the other food sources, initially start with breakfast and watch for an allergic response throughout the day. Eventually, move the meat entree to lunch or dinner.

There are some *warnings* related to meats and babies. Avoid processed meats that are high in sodium and any meat with a casing, such as hotdogs and sausages. Becoming nutritionally wise requires that you read all the labels and understand what types of meats your are offering.

Another good source of protein is the yolk of an egg, but since the egg white is not recommended for babies under a year, it makes sense to hold off on eggs entirely until after a baby's first birthday. Also wait at least a year to introduce peanut butter.

JUICES

Clear liquid fruit juices are not only the last food options to become part of your baby's diet, but the least necessary. Juices offer very little nutritional value and because of their sweetness, should be diluted 50–75 percent with water. If you do offer juices, do so occasionally during the week, instead of every day. Finally, avoid any juice containing pulp, like orange or grapefruit juice.

The U. S. Food and Drug Administration wants consumers to know there is a difference between fruit juices and fruit drinks. Fruit juices are labeled 100% fruit juice with no additives. Fruit drinks only have a percentage of fruit juice, supplemented with added sugars and sulfates. Your baby should not have any fruit drinks until he is well into his toddler years; and even then, they should be pasteurized fruit drinks.

There is an alternative to packaged drinks. Try making your own fresh-fruit treats. Apples, pears, kiwis and grapes blended to a sauce texture are refreshing, healthy and enjoyed by all children.

MAKING YOUR OWN BABY FOOD

Preparing your own baby food is an easy, money-saving alternative to store-bought brands. If you decide to try this, be sure you use organic foods, since they contain no nitrites derived from soil fertilizers. Nitrites have been linked to a type of anemia in babies.

To prepare carrots, peas or green beans, boil in water until tender. Puree in a blender, adding small amounts of purified water as needed. To prepare yams, sweet potatoes or squash, cook them in the oven until very soft. Remove skin and seeds, and puree the remainder in a blender with purified water.

When preparing quantities for freezing, always sterilize your containers. When needed, thaw the food in your refrigerator or microwave, not on the counter.

Cookbooks are a good resource for baby-food preparation and much safer than Internet resources. Books have to be screened and edited before being published. Anyone can post their ideas—good or bad—on the Internet without accountability. Please be discerning about any advice you find on the Internet.

TRAIN, NOT RETRAIN

Mom and Baby will spend a considerable amount of time together at meals, and that makes each meal an opportunity for training basic life-skills, such as where Baby's hands should be. As you offer his food, hold his hands away from the spoon. He doesn't need to help you with the process, although he will try. As you both move into the second adjustment phase of *Babywise II*, you can teach him to place his hands on the side of the highchair tray, or under the tray on his lap, while he is being fed. More on this later.

We raise the point here to remind you that training proactively is better than training reactively with correction. A child is always better off when parents encourage right behavior instead of chasing after wrong behaviors. For example, the child who lacks self-control with his hands tends to put his fingers in his food, then in his hair; and then he wipes them on his shirt, which results in additional clean up and correction. Mom is forced to react, and her training often takes on a negative tone. It is better that you not allow a behavioral freedom to get established in the first place, if it is one that has to be constantly corrected or restricted. That is not fair to the child, and it will become a source of frustration to Mom. That is why we say: *begin as you mean to go.*

Chapter Five

Waketime Activities

In the building process, whether it be a physical structure or the moral fabric of a human heart, laying a proper foundation is the key to future success. Unfavorable or inadequate training, even as early as six months of age, can weaken or undermine a baby's ability to adapt to changes in the future. This is why the early establishment of right "thought" patterns, which come from healthy habits of behavior, are basic tenets of human potential. It is also why waketime activities during the various *babyhood transition* phases must be understood in terms of a child's developing mind and his need for the proper and productive stimulation of the senses. Parents must give attention to *what* expectations are imparted, and equally, *how* those expectations are imparted.

What will your baby's waketimes consist of, and who will be involved in them? While waketime activities should be a family affair with interactions between Mom, Dad and Baby, there should also be some alone time for Baby, allowing him to be totally absorbed in his own world of discovery. But how do you create a consistent environment of learning, and what do you need to understand when it comes to your baby's waketimes?

DEVELOPMENTAL DEPRIVATION

The term "developmental deprivation" does not refer to a child's being deprived of opportunities to learn, but routinely deprived of the *best* opportunities to learn. There are two views on how learning is fostered during the early months of life. One is the "hands off" approach that encourages parents to act as *facilitators* of all learning, rather than proactively assuming the role as *teachers* who direct their child's thought process. This view comes with a two-fold assumption. First, babies are not capable of learning cause and effect relationships directed by parents; and second, that what they do learn comes as a result of their impetuous and momentary curiosity being granted unrestricted access to anything and everything—whether it is the food on highchair or the knick-knacks on the book case.

There is a two-fold weakness with this approach. First, any meaningful learning that may take place is random and accidental. That is in part due to the second weakness. Non-directed or unrestricted learning environments are usually way outside the context of a pretoddler's developing world. As a result, too many freedoms tend to overwhelm the child's senses, thereby his ability to process useful information. This is what fosters developmental deprivation.

The contrasting view, one that we believe makes most sense, places parents in the role as proactive teachers, creating opportunities to learn in every environment: from the highchair to the playpen to the living room. Babies simply need guidance from their parents and, whether that guidance comes from direction or restriction, what parents are providing is "purpose." All learning must be "purposeful" to have meaning and to encourage the formation of developing patterns of logic.

Pretoddlers need direction and guidance from their parents and must learn correct responses for specific situations, and then learn how to transfer the concept from one setting to another. For example, take the two restrictive phrases: "Do not drop your food," and "Do not touch the stereo." While the actions are different and found in different venues within the home, the desired response to both is the same—submission to parental instruction and leadership. If parents reinforce their instruction in the kitchen, but not in the living room, the child's ability to discriminate between what is expected and what is allowed becomes clouded. In contrast, consistent parental restriction between the two venues encourages in the mind of the child the common connection with parental instruction. These "baby connections" help foster deeper patterns of logic that place the child on the fast-track of learning.

There will be an expanded conversation on this fascinating subject in our Topic Pool, chapter Ten, under the heading *Baby-Proofing and Boundaries*. For now, it is enough to say, waketime activities have a greater purpose than simply Baby passing time between the last feeding and the next nap.

They can promote numerous opportunities to learn. Take advantage of them!

PLANNED LEARNING OPPORTUNITIES

Learning opportunities should be predominantly the result of planning, not chance. Help your child learn by placing him in interesting situations that naturally encourage his curiosity right in your own home. These include:

- structured playtime alone
- time with family members
- free playtime

Structured Playtime Alone

Play serves the learning process! Both structured and non-structured playtimes help your child learn how the world works. Structured playtime is a specific time during the day when your child has time to play by himself. It is best to start in the early months with something as simple as a blanket on the floor where Mom can see Baby, but Baby can not see Mom. This Blanket Time eventually leads to Playpen Time, followed by room Time (18–22 months, a time outside the scope of this book, but it is the focus of the next book in this series, *On Becoming Pretoddlerwise*).

Blanket Time: It may be hard to imagine that a six-month-old, lying on his tummy on a small blanket with a colorful teething ring is doing much more than passing time. To the contrary,

Blanket Time provides a secluded environment that allows Baby to focus and concentrate apart from distracting sights and sounds in the house. Introduce Blanket Time before your baby becomes mobile. With parental persistence and consistency, your baby will learn to stay within the boundaries of the blanket. Although your baby will soon transition to Playpen Time, there will be several occasions when Blanket Time will serve both Mom and Baby well.

Where to Begin

Blanket Time can begin as soon as your baby can hold his head up and manipulate a toy in his hands—as early as four months of age. Start with 5–10 minute increments once a day and stretch the time to a happily-tolerated amount. The beauty of a blanket is its mobility. You can place it just about anywhere in the house or yard where it is convenient for Mom and Dad. Grandparents and others will find it helpful when Baby is over for a visit.

<u>Playpen Time</u>: We do not suggest that you transition to Playpen Time at the exclusion of Blanket Time because both are valuable in a baby's life; but the sooner Playpen Time becomes part of your baby's day, the better. While we will expand on the many benefits of Playpen Time in chapter Ten, we wish to introduce some of the basic ones here. For example, playpens provide a "safe" environment for those times when Mom is putting groceries away, taking a quick shower, or helping another sibling. A playpen can double as a bed when away

from home. It is also a great learning center for Baby, because it allows him to focus and concentrate on a toy, learn to manipulate it with his hands, and discover how it works. The playpen is one piece of baby equipment that can and should be used for the next 12 to 18 months.

Learning Times with Family Members

While enjoying your growing baby, it is important that you find the right balance between playing with him and becoming his sole source of entertainment. If you, as a mom, begin to find that your child clings to you, refuses to go to Dad or siblings, or cries when you leave the room, it may be from not enough time with other family members. Here are a few suggestions to help keep your activities family-centered.

Reading: It is never too early to read to your baby and show him colorful picture books, especially cardboard or plastic ones that he can explore alone. This is a fun activity for older siblings to help with and certainly one that Dad will enjoy. Babies find pleasure in being read to, even long before they can understand the words. The continuous flow of sound, as well as the changes in vocal inflections and facial expressions, attract a child's attention. Nestling your child in your lap when you read further enhances this experience.

Bathing: Bathing is a great opportunity to have fun interacting with your baby. You can sing, talk and ask him questions such as, "Where's Matthew's ear?" and "Where's Matthew's arm?".

Then respond, "Here's Matthew's ear!" (wiggling it) and "Here's Matthew's arm!" (with a playful tug). Attentive play and the different voices of Mom, Dad and older siblings help your baby understand the friendly world of family relationships.

Walking: Taking time for a stroll outside is a great activity for the entire family. By six months of age, your baby becomes fascinated with the treasures of nature. A regular walk is a big adventure for your child and, of course, it is healthy for Mom and Dad as well. Strollers that face outward better serve your baby's developing curiosity than strollers that have Baby facing inward, where they see nothing back the back of the stroller.

Physical Touch: A healthy influence on a child's emotional development is the physical touch that comes through playful activities. Play is an important part of every child's growth, and that includes babies. Lying down on the couch, floor or bed and blowing kisses, tickling and cuddling with your baby deepens the human connection of love and security.

SUMMARY

It is amazing what color combinations you will see in a kaleidoscope. With tiny pieces of colored glass and a few mirrors placed at fixed angles, add some light, and you can create an endless assortment of shapes, colors and designs. The patterns are always changing, and that is what makes this a fascinating toy. Undoubtedly you have noticed how quickly your baby is growing and changing, and how much more alert he is during waketimes. Babies are cute at every age, but when they begin to purposefully interact with you with their smiles, cooing sounds and hand clapping, they are more than cute; they are, like a kaleidoscope, reflecting the light of their developing world. Parents bring light into their child's world by thoughtfully managing what and how their child learns.

Coming up in section Two, we move the clock forward and revisit the three activities of your baby's day, but from the perspective of parenting a nine-month-old. What makes this later *Babywise II* phase so exciting is the cognitive alertness that begins to govern mealtimes and waketimes. Like the kaleidoscope, the color patterns change as your nine-month-old's capacity for learning moves to a whole new level!

Section Two

Your Baby from Nine to Twelve Months

Chapter Six

Finger Foods and Snacks

As we address the feed-wake-sleep activities for section Two (chapters six to Ten), we move the clock forward a few months. What are the major growth changes and challenges for the nine to twelve-month-old, and what can parents expect?

First, parents will discover their child is becoming less and less a baby and more and more a pretoddler—one who is not only more alert, but now driven by a heightened sense of curiosity and need to discover. The budding pretoddler sees an object of interest, perhaps a morsel of food precariously sitting on the edge of his highchair or a shiny knick-knack on the bookcase; and what he sees he usually wants. Add mobility to this mix, and the day-to-day challenges for Mom and Dad multiply. What boundaries will they set or what sensible precautions will they put in place? Here is a fact of early parenting: mobility plus curiosity requires parental vigilance, along with planning and forethought on how their baby's day should be structured. All this is to benefit your child and to maximize his learning.

This section of *Babywise II,* addresses the practical side of planning your baby's day. We will talk about behaviors associated with mealtimes, waketimes and naps; but now, more than ever, show you how every activity in your baby's day is connected. There is no lesson learned in the highchair that is not also, in some form, related to a lesson that can be applied to the living room. That is the good news. The bad news is that any trainable moment missed in one activity carries unintended consequences for the other activities. More than ever, parents need to stay vigilant and in tune with the principle of *developmental connectivity*.

Since mealtime in a highchair is the first activity of each cycle, it is good place to begin our discussion. We have already talked about the introduction of solid foods, but that was during the time when Mom exclusively did the feeding. Now at nine months, something new is about to unfold in the life of your baby. His brain will make a subtle, but rather significant connection, which will impact the rest of his life. This connection is first noticed during mealtime with the introduction of *finger foods*.

FINGER FOODS

Your baby's ability to manipulate food with his fingers is a small, but significant milestone of development. This involves hand-to-mouth coordination with the newly arrived presence of the *raking* and *pincer* reflexes.

In reality, your baby's raking skills have been around a while as demonstrated by the times when playing on a blanket, reaching out to a toy and raking it towards himself using the gross motor skill of arm and hand together. However, it is not until eight or nine months of age that he acquires the ability to *rake* fine objects with his fingers by opening and closing them around the object. He then attempts to bring his whole hand, with the morsels of food inside, to his mouth.

The *pincer reflex* represents the next skill level of finger dexterity. This is when the thumb-forefingers connection is made in the brain allowing your baby to pick up small pieces of food with precision and speed. Both the racking and pincer reflexes signal a major *Babywise II* transition: moving from being fed to feeding oneself. Without that basic skill, a person cannot achieve true independence.

The *pincer reflex* opens up a variety of new finger food options to consider. As a Mom, your first concern is not simply the nutritional value in the finger foods, but also the safety aspect of each food type. Even though most nine-month-old children have a few teeth, the texture of their finger foods should be soft enough to be gummed, not chewed. If you question the safety of a particular food, try placing it in your mouth. Does it dissolve, melt or break up into small pieces without chewing it? If no, wait until your baby is at least a year old before offering it again.

There are many easy-to-handle and fun finger foods for a nine-month-old, including small pieces of cut-up banana, simple cereals like puffed rice, and wafer-type crackers. Eventually, Mom can add well-cooked peas, green beans cut in very small pieces, and bits of cooked potato. Baby-food manufacturers offer a variety of finger-food assortments for stages three and four, and your baby's pediatrician should have a recommended list of age-appropriate foods to offer.

Of course, there are some table and finger foods that are "off limits" until your baby is at least a year old. We mentioned a few of those in our last section, but here is a more complete list:

Foods not to serve in the First Year

- egg whites
- nuts or peanut butter
- honey or other sweeteners
- uncooked vegetables
- whole grapes or cherry tomatoes
- raw berries such as raspberries or blackberries unless you take the time to cut them into tiny pieces

Be aware that the more solid foods your baby eats, the more his stools will change. The stools normally become firmer and change color. For example, beets will turn stools reddish and peas will make them greenish. Unfortunately, for those doing diaper changes, the strong, unpleasant odor of ordinary human stools will become commonplace for the next year or more.

Sending a Mixed Message?

As adults, we do not tend to think about the conflicting messages that can accompany the introduction of finger foods when it comes to who is in control. For example, Mom and Dad are in control when offering food on a spoon, but Baby is asked to be in control once finger foods are introduced. Is this a mixed message? From a ten-month-old's perspective, it might be! One moment Mom is saying, "Here is your finger food, help yourself." The next moment she is saying, "Put your hands on the side of the tray. Do not touch your food." How can a parent resolve this tension?

One way is for Mom to serve the spoon items first (vegetables and fruits) and then to offer the finger foods. The time between the items served delineates what the child can and cannot touch. A second option has Mom using a dish with compartments, allowing the food to be separated—pureed foods on one side that mom will serve and finger foods on the other side from which baby can serve himself. Mom maintains control of the dish which serves as the boundary. As you are probably beginning to discover, concepts learned during mealtime are usually transferable to other activities during the day. *Begin as you mean to go!*

SNACKS

Snacks are a fun treat but are usually reserved for the 11 or 12-month-old. Veteran moms will tell you that offering too many snacks at the wrong times encourages poor eating habits and sets the stage for a picky eater. If you see this happening cut back on the snacks. Here are a few helpful hints about snacking:

1. Snacks are not needed every day.

2. Moderation is key; do not let snacks detract from a hearty appetite.
3. Do not use food to avoid conflict.
4. Avoid using food as a pacifier.
5. The place for snacking should be consistent, such as in the highchair; avoid letting your child wander the house freely during snack time.
6. Consider offering a snack in the afternoon, when Baby wakes from his nap.

THE PICKY EATER

Like all people, your baby will show preferences in taste. While you will occasionally offer the foods he enjoys, there will come a time when he must learn to eat what the rest of the family enjoys. This should be a natural food transition as your baby moves from commercial baby food to table food. We tend to believe that picky eaters are more often created by a parent's lack of resolve or insistence about a food choice than any other factor.

Just as you did when first introducing solids, if you experience any strong resistance toward a particular taste or texture, stop and wait a few weeks; then try again. It is not unusual for pretoddlers to acquire a taste for the foods they may have rejected just a few weeks earlier. Persistence does pay off, and your baby will be less likely to become a picky eater in the future

Finally, try to make mealtime a pleasant experience for everyone in the family. Some of the most wonderful memories of life come from times shared as a family around the dinner table. While we place books, computers, plants and newspapers on the kitchen table, its most important use is when family members congregate at mealtimes. Here are age-appropriate suggestions to help make your mealtimes a joyful family experience.

For children under 6 months: When possible, place your baby in his infant seat near the dinner table. Being able to see and hear his family interacting helps establish an early family connection. When it is just Mom or Dad, get into the habit of talking with your baby during mealtime. While there might be occasions when your baby is in the playpen or sleeping during a family meal, try to keep him at the table with the family.

6–12 months (or until self-feeding): At this age, your baby may eat his main meal before the rest of the family sits down. Then, while the family enjoys their meal together, he can sit in his highchair with a toy or some finger foods. Now, everyone is participating at dinner time!

12 months and up: To keep evening mealtimes pleasant, put more concentrated effort into working on highchair challenges during the other mealtimes, such as breakfast and lunch. This does not mean you will not correct during dinner, but the extra effort put into training the baby at the other meals will speed up the process of his learning and achieving mealtime harmony when everyone is sitting together. We expand on this topic in our next book, *On Becoming Pretodderwise, Parenting Your 12–18 Month Old.*

WEANING YOUR BABY

Weaning, by definition, is the process by which parents offer food supplements in place of, or in addition to, mother's milk. This process begins the moment you give your baby formula or when he first tastes cereal. From that moment on, weaning is a gradual process.

From the Breast

The duration of breastfeeding depends on Mom and Baby's mutual desires and needs. No one can say for sure what age is ideal for your unique situation. For some it may be six months, for others a year or more. (A year is a very achievable goal for most moms.) Breastfeeding beyond a year is a matter of preference rather than a nutritional requirement since adequate supplementary food is available.

You can begin weaning by eliminating one nursing period at a time, waiting three to four days before dropping the next one. This time frame allows Mom's body to make the proper adjustment in her milk production. The late-afternoon feeding is usually the easiest to drop since it is a busy time of the day. Replace each feeding with 6–8 ounces of formula or cow's milk only if your baby is at least a year old. If your baby is nine months or older, we suggest using a sippy cup rather than a bottle. This transition will be easier if you have introduced the cup prior to weaning.

Once your baby moves into the pretoddler phase, he requires at least 1,000 calories a day for normal growth. Some of those calories should come from 16–24 ounces of whole milk. Wait until your child is two years old before introducing low-fat milk.

From the Bottle

By the time your baby is a year old, he can begin to wean from his bottle to a sippy cup. Begin by eliminating the bottle at one meal, substituting the cup. Do this for another meal and then another until the transition is complete. This may take anywhere from two weeks to a month. Mom and Dad should be the ones setting the timetable for this transition, not Baby.

We will close this section with a reminder. Introducing solids to your baby's diet is natural part of his growth and development. Stay mindful of proactively training your baby to avoid retraining later: *begin as you mean to go.*

Chapter Seven

Babyhood Training & More

During the first two years of life, a child has very little understanding of what his basic needs are, or how well Mom and Dad are actually meeting those needs. That is not so bad for the child since he is not responsible for seeing that his life runs smoothly. His parents, however, are responsible not only for moment-by-moment care, but also for their influence on his future behavior. As is true with every generation, parents are society's representatives and are expected to bring their little ones into reasonable behavioral conformity. The early process of this sobering truth usually requires an understanding of the *When, How, What* and *Why* of training.

- *When* refers to training that is age appropriate: When will I train?

- *How* addresses the process of early training: How will I train?
- *What* speaks to the priorities of training: What will I train?
- *Why* provides the greater purpose of training: Why will I train?

Once your baby crosses the threshold of nine months of age, your training will be more purposeful because it becomes more specific. This is partly due to your baby's ability to regulate his behavior to a wide range of parental expectations, and this is no small thing! Your pretoddler is in a growth period when he can actually choose to comply or not comply with Mom or Dad's basic instructions. This new awareness opens the doorway to multiple opportunities for Mom and Dad to train, from times in the highchair to play times in the living room.

Speaking of Training

Once the *pincer reflex* is mastered, a baby is on his way to self-feeding, which is also a step toward independence. However, the newly-acquired motor skill of grasping small items in the highchair is a developmental connection that can also be applied in living room, where items once out of reach are now viewed, by the mobile pretoddler, as trophies to be gained. This changes the game for Mom and Dad because a pretoddler's mobility, plus curiosity, creates a sense of urgency for Mom and Dad that requires a working understanding of the three components of training: *instruction, encouragement* and *correction*.

When speaking to a group of young parents, we often see smiles and affirming nods while discussing the practical side of parental instruction or the persuasive power of encouragement. However, once the conversation changes to the topic of pretoddler correction, facial expressions turn to bewilderment. Having been around young parents, we certainly can understand how a parent of a nine-month-old might find a conversation about correction slightly premature and outside the context of their present circumstances. Yet, the value of correction cannot be dismissed or underestimated when you have a mobile pretoddler in the home. Their safety depends on such parental interaction. Let's talk about this.

During pretoddler months, behaviors needing correction are wrong *functionally*, but not *morally*. Young children need correction for inappropriate and unsafe actions, but at these tender ages, parents are dealing with issues related to the child's "nature" more than any sense of right and wrong. In fact, your pretoddler has no sense of right and wrong because this is a function of the "higher conscience," which is a few years away from being developed. Infants and pretoddlers think and act with a single focus of *"me, myself* and *I."* nonetheless, this basic "me-ism" must, in time, be replaced with a more harmonious family "we-ism" if there is any hope of taming and training the budding ego.

Training is a positive term that means to "initiate, set patterns or cause one to learn." You do not want to prevent your child from exploring life, but you do want to provide reasonable guidance in the process. Part of that guidance includes correcting wrong patterns and encouraging right ones. If you neglect or underestimate the need for corrective measures during these highly impressionable pretoddler months, your little one could possibly enter early childhood with behavioral deficits. Playing catch-up in behavior is never easy.

The process of training during babyhood months is a balancing act. Like a three-legged stool, it can stand firm only as long as each leg stays intact and sits even with the other two. Again, the three legs of training are *instruction, encouragement* and *correction*:

- *instruct* to introduce parental expectations
- *encourage* to reinforce the value of parental expectations
- *correct* to restore the child back to parental expectations

PRETODDLER INSTRUCTION: WHAT DOES IT LOOK LIKE?

One of the first principles of giving instructions is to make sure they are aligned with the child's age and ability to understand and comply. A mom might reasonably instruct her three-year-old to return to his room and put away his puzzle; but those same instructions would be too lofty for a 12-month-old. And yet, going in the opposite direction, many time parents hold back their instructions believing their pretoddler is not old enough to understand. However, we know from experience that pretoddlers tend to understand more than we think. This is in part because the comprehension of the spoken word proceeds the other two vocabulary skill levels, speaking and reading. Here is how the three levels of vocabulary comprehension develop.

Level 1: *Understanding*. A baby understands the meaning of words long before he can verbalize them. An eight-month-old, for example, will wave bye-bye or play pat-a-cake when encouraged to do so. By the first year, a child has an enormous understanding of vocabulary, and he demonstrates this by his responses to instructions such as "come to Mama," "sit down," "Blow kisses," or "Touch the kitty." Your child is responding with understanding, but not with the spoken word just yet.

Level 2: *Speaking*. Around his first birthday, your pretoddler will begin to babble to a toy or a family member. Although you may not understand what he is saying, his babbling means something to him. These "word thoughts" coming out in scrambled speech represent his attempt to communicate with language. In time he will begin to recognize simple words that he can form on his lips, such as "Da Da" or "Ma Ma."

Level 3: *Reading*. At this level of vocabulary comprehension you child begins to associate letters with short words, primarily nouns often heard in picture books: bunny, lamb, horse, dog, and cat are the most common. Reading comprehension begins during the preschool years. (For an expanded explanation of language development, see Appendix A.)

These three levels of vocabulary comprehension support a pretoddler's readiness to learn and retain. As a Mom and Dad, are you ready to train?

LEARN TO SPEAK LIFE-PROMOTING WORDS

Think about how the people who most influenced you used their words. Did their words promote "life" or "death;" did they build you up or tear you down? Moving the clock forward to the present, if someone recorded your family conversations, what would the playback sound like? Does your speech focus more on what your child is doing wrong and what he should not do, than on what he is doing right and what he should be doing?

Recently, a first-time mom was working through screaming issues with her 12-month-old. While sitting in the highchair, little emily would protest loudly with bouts of screaming, whenever she felt her mom was taking too much time serving her food. Frustrated, emily's mom raised her voice over the noise, imploring emily to: "Stop screaming!" "Settle down!" "Stop fussing!"

Although Mom was hoping to achieve some mealtime peace with her instructions, in actuality she was losing ground. What parent has not done this? Mom focused her instructions more on what Emily was doing wrong, instead of pointing to the virtue she desired Emily to mimic. She was eager to suppress the screaming, but offered no substitute for it.

Fortunately, we were dealing with a very teachable parent who turned the challenges into moments of positive training by employing the "life" principle. By saying gently, "Be patient, Emily, Mommy is coming," she was pointing to the virtue she desired to instill into Emily's thinking. Positive, life-giving words replaced negative, discouraging words. The virtues Mom hoped Emily would employ, "patience" and "gentleness," replaced the vice she was originally attempting to suppress, which was Emily's out-of-control screaming.

When parents focus only on their children's wrong behavior, then the right behavior they are hoping to instill is left undefined. That eventually translates into a child who learns to avoid *what not to do,* rather than *what he should do*.

From our experience, learning to speak "life" is more of a challenge for Mom and Dad than it is for the children. We invite you as a reader to think back to your own upbringing. As a child, did you ever hear instructions such as, "Do not spill your milk on the way to the table"? That statement can easily be turned around to the positive simply by saying, "Let's see how carefully you can carry your milk to the table." One statement attempts to discourage wrong, while the other statement attempts to encourage right.

While the difference here might appear minor, over the life of your child, negative and positive words have a cumulative effect, because such words shape a child's outlook about self, others, and about life. Learn to speak life to your pretoddler by instructing in what you want him to do instead of what you do not want him to do.

SPEAKING YOUR PRETODDLER'S NAME

Directing your pretoddler with specific instructions works well. Instructions such as, "Place your hands on the side of the highchair," and "Keep your food on your tray please," will get your message across. But there is a more effective way to communicate the same instructions—include your child's name. For example, "Matthew, place your hands on the side of the highchair." Because Matthew is *me-oriented* by nature, saying his name draws attention to the specific task you're desiring of him.

Think about it. When we point out a fun object, we naturally begin with a name: "Matthew, look at the balloon," and "Look Matthew, a butterfly!" We do that because we want the child we are addressing to focus on what we are pointing out. There is something in your child's name that helps draw attention to your voice. The same principle works when your are giving instructions.

A WORD "FITLY SPOKEN"

Encouragement, as we previously noted, reinforces the value and worth of parental instruction. What does encouragement look like to a 10 or 12-month-old? There is an old Jewish proverb that goes something like this: "A word fitly spoken is like apples of gold in settings of silver." There is something inspiring about the timing of those words. Try to think of encouragement as words "fitly spoken" into the lives of children. Encouragement confirms a behavior and inspires its continuation. Who does not enjoy a pat on the back or hearing, "Well done!" from someone we respect? Our children are no different. They are encouraged when justified praise comes their way.

Little people especially enjoy praise with enthusiasm. They love to hear Mom, Dad or their siblings get excited over something they did or did not do. For example, ten-month-old Micah was aware of a small bookcase with three shelves. The upper shelves supported some books and DVDs belonging to his older siblings. Micah knew those shelves were off limits to his hands, so when his parents observed his amazing restraint, they encouraged him with an enthusiastic, "Good boy, Micah! You're playing with Micah's toys."

What Micah tuned into was not so much the words (although they do matter), but the enthusiastic tone of the words. When he is ready to touch something off-limits in the living room, he hears a different tone: "M-i-cah!" Here the tone is a warning with a clear message. As he moves away, he then hears an enthusiastic, "Good job, Micah! You obeyed Mommy."

True encouragement motivates right behavior; do not underestimate the power of it. If we are not verbalizing our encouragement to our children or spouse, we are still sending a message, but what kind of message?

TEACH BASIC SIGN LANGUAGE TO YOUR BABY

Sign language is truly a universal language. It works in all cultures at all times, and for all age groups. Teaching basic sign language is a wonderful way to bridge the gap in your baby's life between vocabulary comprehension and the spoken word. So often a one-year-old sitting in a highchair will become frustrated and begin to scream for what he wants. While screaming is a form of communication, there is a better alternative. Teach your pretoddler how to communicate by using sign language. Start with the basic sign for "Please."

Why start with "please"? Because "please" is one of the first acts of voluntary submission a child will give to his parents' leadership. It is the first courtesy and virtue that makes sense to your child and will motivate him to do other courtesies. It is also very easy to teach. At each mealtime, just before offering your six-month-old his first taste of food, take his hand through the motions of signing "please" while saying, "Let's do please." each time you take his little hand across his chest, you are imprinting a basic courtesy that will become part of his life. The more consistent you are, the sooner Baby associates signing please with receiving something he enjoys. Like all good investments, a worthy return will soon follow.

If you begin teaching your seven-month-old "please," he may be voluntarily giving it back to you in a few weeks or months—but it will eventually happen! One day he will see something he wants, look at you, and his little hand will begin to sign "please," knowing this action brings rewards.

PLEASE

(Place right hand over heart and pull back across the chest toward right arm.)

Over time you can add "thank you," "more," "all done," and "stop." (See more signing illustrations at the end of this chapter.) Once your child reaches a year and has demonstrated understanding of how to sign but refuses to do so, use natural consequences to reinforce the correct response. If he wants a toy but refuses to sign "please," withhold the toy. If it is a cookie, withhold the cookie reminding him each time to say "please" and the cookie is his. Do not get into a power struggle at mealtimes, and never withhold a meal because your pretoddler refuses to sign. But do stay consistent and persistent; the rewards are many.

Here are a few more reasons for teaching basic sign language to your pretoddler:

- You are teaching and reinforcing habits of self-control.
- You are helping to eliminate wrong forms of communication by providing right modes of expression.
- You are aiding discretionary correction in the future. There will be times when you cannot easily or appropriately correct your child publicly or verbally. The silence of signing, together with Mom's facial expression, communicates the same intent as verbal correction.
- You are teaching your child a second language during a time in his life when he is most receptive to language formation.

Will My Baby Understand?

Do not be surprised if one day you take your baby's hand to sign "please" with him and begin to feel resistance as you work through the motion. This probably means your child understands what you are requiring and has decided, "I do not want to do this." We recently received a note from a *Babywise* Mom who shared her surprised when her nine-month-old daughter openly resisted Mom's attempts to guide her through the "please" sign:

"I was surprised when she resisted and actually tried to fight me. I realized this was one of the first battles that, as a mother, I must win. I stayed with it and in two week's time, my daughter was willingly and happily signing 'please' when she wanted something. Even more amazing was the lesson I learned: my child's surrender gave way to her own happiness. Now that she is 20 months old, she signs 'please,' 'thank you,' 'more,' 'all done,' 'Mommy,' 'Daddy,' and 'I love you.' All of this is in addition to her developing verbal skills."

This child's ability to communicate amazed both her parents and other people who came into contact with her. Early sign-training pays dividends now and will in the future. Have fun!

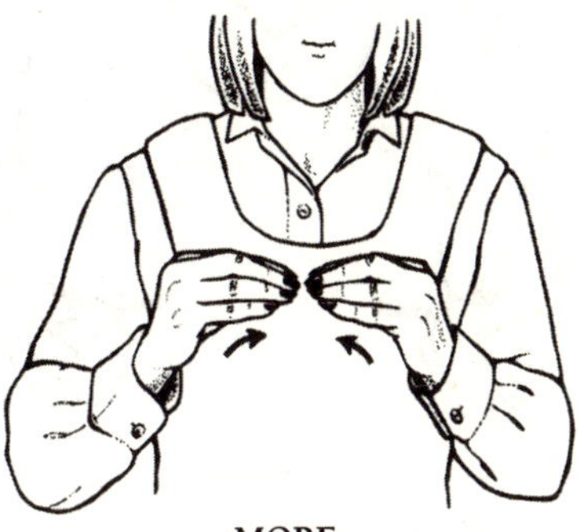

MORE

Use both hands, bring finger tips together and tap twice

THANK YOU

Place tips of the hand (fingers together) against the mouth and throw hand forward, similar to blowing a kiss.

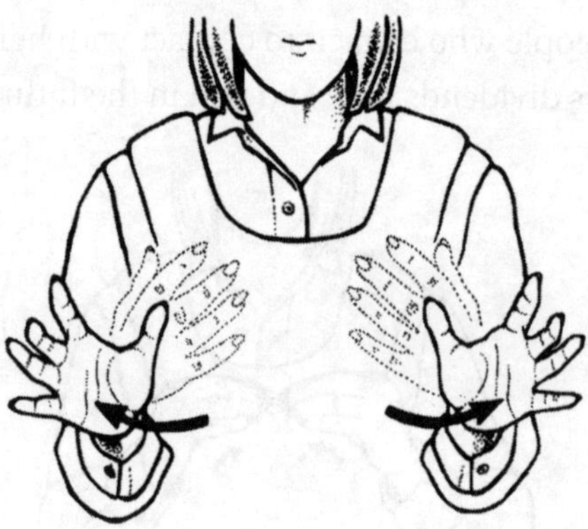

ALL DONE

Put hands in front of you with fingers spread apart. Turn hands back and forth.

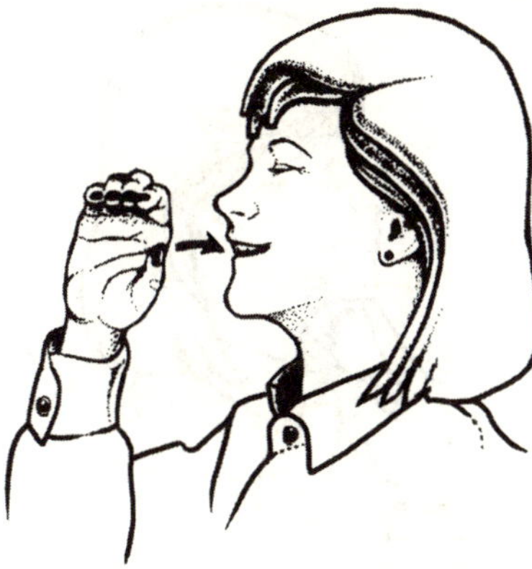

DRINK

Place your hand in the shape of a "C" in front of mouth, thumb resting on chin, and bring hands up as if pouring a drink into the mouth.

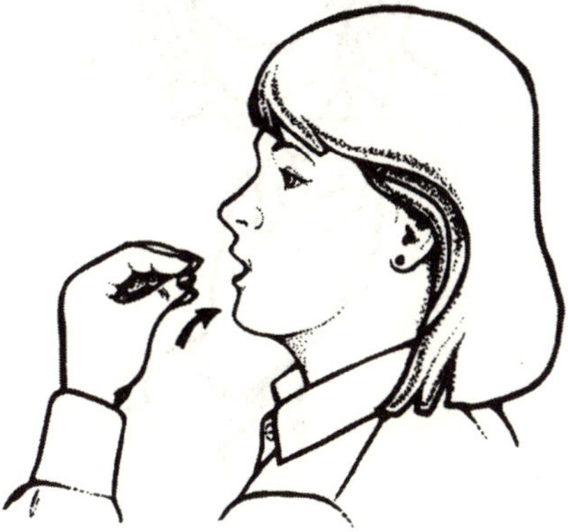

EAT

All fingertips resting on thumb, bring hand toward mouth a couple of times.

THIRSTY

Slide tip of the index finger down the front of neck.

HUNGRY

With hand in the shape of a "C," place it just below the throat, palm facing in, and bring it down.

MOMMY

With fingers spread apart, thumb touches middle of chin.

DADDY

With fingers spread apart, thumb touches middle of forehead.

YES

Close hand, nod hand at wrist up and down.

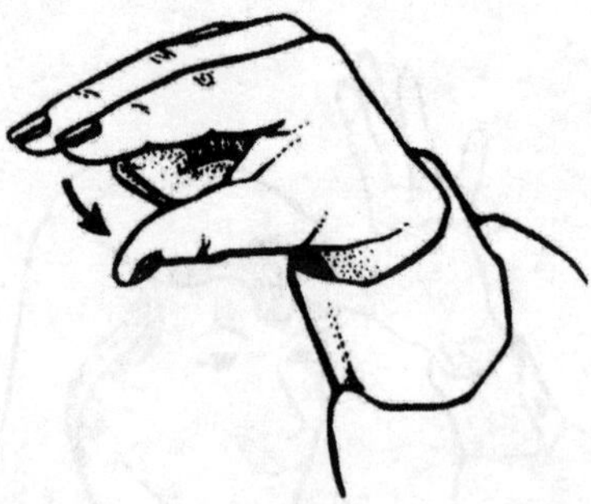

NO

Bring index finger and middle finger together to rest on thumb in one "snapping" motion.

Chapter Eight

The Meaning of Correction

Some parents might find a conversation about correction of pretoddlers difficult to reconcile. After all, what malicious misdeed is a ten-month-old capable of doing that would call for corrective measures? unfortunately, confusion exists because the terms, "correction," "consequences," and "punishment" are often interchanged as if they all mean the same thing. They don't! Please take note of this flow chart.

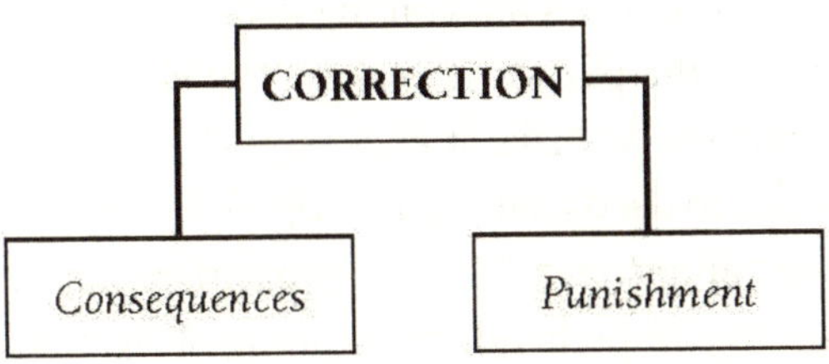

Most pretoddler correction involves fairly innocent behaviors, although the behaviors themselves are potentially dangerous or destructive. For example, a crawling ten-month-old is curious about everything—the shiny figurines on the bookcase, how long the plant vine can stretch before breaking, where the stairs lead, or how much food can be dropped on the floor; before Mom notices. While these actions are wrong "practically," they are not motivated out of a little heart seeking to maliciously do something wrong. (That will come in time, but not for a few years.) Yet, unintentional wrong behaviors still need to be corrected. As noted, the purpose of correction is to restore a child back to the right pathway of behavior, because he is heading in the wrong direction. This can be done through encouragement, and it can be done by using age-appropriate consequences; but it should not be done with punishment. *Never!*

Consequences and punishment are independent subcategories of correction. Consequences are tied to specific actions, while punishment is tied to a belief system. The ten-month-old who continues to drop the same toy out of his playpen, only to have Mom fetch it for him, learns to play "mommy fetch." The child who drops the same toy and loses it for the duration of his playpen time learns the consequences of his action. The toy is not coming back!

In contrast, the purpose of *punishment* is to set a value on wrong behavior—to make it expensive. Punishment should always be tied to deeds that are morally right and wrong. That is why true "punishment" is not appropriate until a child is old enough to comprehend the meaning of right and wrong.

That will not happen until the formation of conscience, which emerges around three years of age. The conclusion? You do not punish a baby. Pretoddlers and toddlers do plenty of unsafe and unwise things, and that is why during the *Babywise II* phase, the battles are not over right and wrong as much as health, safety and keeping the child on track. For that parents can train through consequences.

Having made the distinction between corrections in general, consequences, and punishment, we can now move to specific waketime activities and the challenges common to this age group.

HIGHCHAIR CHALLENGES

Waketime challenges will come throughout the day, and many of them will show up while your little one is sitting in his highchair. While the offenses listed differ in specific actions, the method of correction for each offense is often the same. Included in the group of common highchair violations are:

- flipping the plate
- dropping and throwing food
- playing with food
- placing messy hands in his hair
- banging on the tray
- standing in the highchair
- arching his back
- blowing bubbles with his food ("blowing raspberries")
- screaming

The behaviors listed share two things in common: they come during mealtime, and they happen when the child is sitting in the highchair. Since eliminating mealtime is not an option, you will have to work on eliminating the highchair challenges. Let's consider two examples—flipping the plate and the intentional dropping of food from the highchair.

Train—Do Not Retrain

Parents should place finger foods either directly on the clean highchair tray or on a plate. When finger foods are on a plate, one common and curious temptation all babies attempt at one time or another, is to flip the plate. That might work out well for the puppy around the house, but not so good for Mom. This is the time for correction; but what type of correction is age appropriate? Here are four options.

1. Verbal Correction: Direct your little one with your voice, speaking firmly but not harshly. Sometimes an elevated tone will be necessary to get your child's immediate attention, but realize an earnest or urgent tone is not the same as a harsh tone. Accompany your verbal correction with your hand or finger directed to the area of violation. For example, if your little one is intentionally dropping food from his highchair, take his little hand and hold it away from the food while saying, "Matthew, no! Do not drop your food." If Matthew is blowing bubbles with his food, place your finger over his mouth with slight pressure and state firmly, "Matthew, no! Keep your food in your mouth." The same principle applies if Matthew's little hands are about to touch something in the living room that you deemed off limits.

2. *A light-to-moderate squeeze to the hand*: Parents find this second method very effective because discomfort, even in a mild form, attracts attention faster than anything else. The intent is not to cause pain for the purpose of punishment, but to gain your child's attention, so you can train him to your reasonable mealtime expectations. Using a slight squeeze to gain attention will not leave your child psychologically damaged, affect self-esteem, train him to hit other children, teach him violence, or cause him in adulthood to abuse his own children. How often educators are tempted to think in extremes to avoid the obvious or the uncomfortable! society depends on parents to instill in their children a healthy sense of self-restriction, and that is not as hard as some people make it out to be.

3. *Loss of a privilege or toy*: Taking away a related privilege, such as dessert, or a favorite after-mealtime plaything is a logical consequence that trains effectively. The purpose of logical consequences is to reinforce your verbal instructions. For example, let's say your child is now 13 months of age and clearly understands what "please" means, and what Mom expects. He points to something he desires but refuses to sign or say, "please." Withholding the item until he complies, is not only a logical consequence of a decision in his control, but also a strong motivator for him to submit to your values.

4. <u>*Isolation in the crib or playpen*</u>: Isolation removes your child from the act or place of conflict. Your baby will probably fuss, but he will very quickly make the connection between his action (or inaction) and your instructions. After some time of isolation, try bringing him back to the highchair or wherever the problem took place, and see if the lesson was learned. If it was, encourage him with words of praise; if not, tomorrow will bring other training opportunities.

Parents will inquire if using the crib for sleep and a place of isolation could cause confusion for a ten-month-old. No worries, it doesn't. Even babies can distinguish the difference between a time of correction and a time for sleep.

<u>Note</u>: spanking, as traditionally practiced in society, is not an appropriate form of correction during the pretoddler phase of development. Parents can achieve what they need to by using verbal correction, squeezing the hand, loss of privilege and appropriate isolation.

SUMMARY

Whether it is a mealtime or living-room challenge, one thing is certain: immediate and consistent consequences speed up the learning process. In the past, educators were concerned with parents who pushed their children too fast. Today, we are concerned with parents who do not push their children fast enough when it comes to basic life skills, such as motivating self-control.

Chapter Nine

Naps and Nighttime Sleep

As stated in *Babywise,* where there is ability, there is a natural capacity. Your baby has already demonstrated both the natural capacity and ability to sleep through the night, which is an acquired skill resulting from training. This chapter focuses on sleep-related activities and the various sleep transitions. Later in this chapter we answer the most common nap and sleep questions related to this stage of growth.

THE SLEEP TRANSITIONS

Stable sleep patterns are tied back to routine and predictable feed-wake-sleep rhythms established early on. However, if there are a number of disruptions in your baby's eating or waketime patterns, there will be corresponding changes in his sleep patterns. Stay on top of this by being as consistent as possible with mealtime and naptime. Sleep is an important part of a baby's life, and it will continue to be throughout the toddler years.

Dropping the Late Afternoon Nap

Young children need daytime rest. For the *Babywise* mom the procedure is fairly simple. When naptime comes, Baby goes down. Not much will change over the next 12 months. At five months of age, the average *PDF* baby takes two 1½ to 2-hour naps and an additional catnap in the late afternoon. Between six and eight months of age, his sleep needs decrease as his waketime increases. This is especially noticeable in babies who sleep 10 to 12 hours at night. The sleep center in a baby's brain begins to send a wake-up signal if there is too much sleep in a 24-hour period. That is when you know your baby is ready to drop his afternoon catnap. Here are three common signs:

1. Your baby begins waking in the middle of the night.
2. Your baby is waking very early in the morning.
3. Your baby is routinely waking early during one or both daytime naps, possibly sleeping only 45 minutes.

Be cautious, however, the signs above are not exclusively associated with nap transitions. Other factors may mirror those symptoms, including hunger, sickness, and possibly teething. Consider all the probabilities before acting on any single factor. If you believe the sign is sleep related, drop the catnap first. This sleep transition may also require that you create a longer morning waketime by pushing the morning nap back 30–45 minutes.

Your baby will continue with two naps a day until the next sleep transition: when he drops the morning nap, which usually occurs between 15–24 months of age. We discuss this particular nap transition in the next book of this series, *On Becoming Pretoddlerwise: Parenting Your 12–18 Month Old*.

There are other reasons your baby will wake up before achieving a full nap. He might be ready to start solids, have a soiled diaper, or have an arm or leg stuck in a crib slat. This is when parental assessment is needed and possibly a quick glance at chapter six in *Babywise* where we discussed the many influences on nap disturbances.

If you cannot readily discern why your baby is waking early, try gently patting his back for a few moments, reassuring him that you are present, or picking him up and cuddling him while whispering softly to him. Hearing Mom or Dad's calming voice during a time of stress is very reassuring. After he is calm, gently return him to the crib. If he continues to fuss, maybe naptime is over for today. If this is the option you choose, simply readjust his schedule for the rest of the day and monitor tomorrow's sleep times.

The Fatigued Baby

A tired baby can usually recoup needed sleep in one good nap or at least within a 24-hour cycle. A fatigued baby, however, fights sleep, yet has a disruption in sleep cycles that requires special attention. If you respond by keeping your baby up, letting him skip his naps, the problem will only intensify. If you attempt to force sleep on him by not responding to his cries (legitimately born out of fatigue), Mom and Dad can quickly become emotional wrecks, and Baby will not be helped.

Let's look into the context and uniqueness of this challenge. For the *Babywise* family, healthy sleep has two primary components that most moms are unwilling to give up: a baby who sleeps through his naps without waking and who sleeps in his crib for those naps. While both are important, one must be temporarily suspended for the greater good of the baby—the restoration of his natural sleep rhythms.

Infant fatigue is much like adult fatigue. We all know what it feels like to be so tired that you can't sleep. That is because fatigue attacks our sleep rhythms, preventing us from entering the ebb and flow of active and relaxed sleep states. For a baby, it may be the result of his routine being out of whack for several days, especially during naptime. Mom's priority here is to find a stress-free solution that reestablishes her baby's circadian rhythm.

If you suspect your baby's nap challenge is fatigue and you are now in a position to get him back into a predictable routine, we suggest you find a comfortable chair and a good book, and allow your baby to take his nap in your arms. This naptime procedure might extend into the next day, but Baby should return to the crib for his naps by the third day if not sooner.

This temporary adjustment works because the tension between the need for sleep and the appropriate place for sleep is temporarily suspended, so your baby can receive his necessary restorative sleep. You are not creating a "sleep prop" because this sleep adjustment is only for a couple days, but you are satisfying his sleep needs by helping him overcome his fatigue.

Prevention of course, is the best medicine and always will be, so try to think how your perfect sleeper became a fatigued baby; because it did not just happen! One day's suspension of a baby's routine will not foster the condition of fatigue. Take a look at what is going on in your home and with the baby's schedule, and make the appropriate adjustments.

Do not take this sleep challenge lightly. Optimal alertness comes from optimal sleep. It is during times of optimal alertness that your baby's brain grows and develops. Poor sleep habits negatively impact the brain's neuro-chemical transmitters that stimulate growth.

Nighttime Sleep

At six months of age, your baby's nighttime sleep patterns should be well-established. An average of 10–12 hours of continuous sleep is the norm. That pattern will change little over the next few years except for a few temporary disruptions from sickness or daytime nap transitions.

SLEEP PROPS AND PROBLEMS

Sleep is a natural function of the body. The primary cue for infant sleep is sleepiness. Some sleep props or aids, such as a special blanket or stuffed animal, are usually harmless; while others, such as the nighttime bottle, pacifier and thumb-sucking, can be addictive. The problem is not getting the child to fall asleep initially, but training him to fall back to sleep without the prop. Let's take a closer look.

The Bottle

Too many children become conditioned to going to bed with a bottle and depend on it to fall asleep. You can avoid the bottle prop by not getting in the habit of putting your baby down with one—and spare your child dental problems down the road. This does not mean he will never take a bottle in his crib. There may be an occasional nap when Baby, bottle and crib form a convenient alliance for a busy mom. As long as this behavior does not become a habit, it will not become addictive.

The Blanket

To keep your child from becoming overly attached to one blanket, consider limiting its use to the crib or bed and on some occasions, a long car ride. Do not let your baby or pretoddler drag it everywhere he goes. Help him learn that true security is tied to relationships, especially with Mom and Dad, not objects.

The Pacifier

There are many good reasons for using a pacifier with your newborn, but by six months of age, any need for non-nutritive sucking is greatly diminished. Does your child need a pacifier to fall asleep? If so, now is the time to start breaking that habit.

Obviously it will be easier to remove the pacifier at six months than at 12–18 months of age. It works best to remove it gradually. Start with one "pacifier-free" nap and eventually move to the other naps, and then nighttime. Expect some crying, but remind yourself that it will be temporary. Another suggestion is to pierce the pacifier with a needle and release the vacuum. The vacuum bubble is what makes the pacifier enjoyable; when the bubble is gone, the pleasure is decreased, often resulting in the child weaning himself from the pacifier. This suggestion can be applied to the six-month-old or sixteen-month-old.

SUDDEN AND UNEXPLAINABLE CRYING

It's scary! Your baby cries as if in pain but you do not know why. First, you check his forehead for any indication of a fever. Ears and nose are next. No redness is good news, so you examine your baby's mouth for an emerging tooth. Nothing there; examination time is over.

Not so fast! There is something else to check: your child's fingers and toes. Toe-tourniquet syndrome is when a single strand of hair, usually Mom's, or a fiber from a shagged carpet where Baby was playing, somehow gets wrapped around a toe or finger. Although hardly noticeable, it eventually tightens and cuts off circulation to the appendage, causing swelling and pain. The problem is often missed because Baby is usually wearing socks or a sleeper. While this does not explain every sudden and unexplainable cry, it alerts you to the need for a daily once-over of your baby's body.

QUESTIONS ABOUT PRETODDLER SLEEP

A few disruptions can turn a great nap and nighttime sleeper into a challenging child. Rest assured, most of these challenges have an explanation and can be quickly brought under control. These are the most common sleep challenges for *Babywise II* babies:

1. Our six-month-old has always slept through the night. Now, all of a sudden, he is waking and crying. Why is this happening? What should we do?

This is a common problem between five and eight months. While your *Babywise* books provides a large number of specific reasons for a baby waking early, here are four general causes:

<u>One</u>: The first reason is hunger. His waking may signal that he is going through a growth spurt. If you suspect this is the case, add another one to two nursing periods during the day or try supplementing with a bottle after breastfeeding to see if this solves the problem. The early waking might also mean that your baby is ready for solid foods, or that your milk supply is falling behind his nutritional needs.

<u>Two</u>: It may be time to drop the late-afternoon nap. With three full naps a day, your baby's body may be sending signals that he is getting too much sleep.

<u>Three</u>: Teething or sickness affect sleep. This is easier to identify since daytime irritability usually accompanies these conditions.

Four: Has there been a major change in your baby's daytime routine? Has this been a busy week? Did you just start a new job? Is your baby being overly entertained by friends and relatives or co-workers to the point that naps are being skipped? Overly-tired babies will be fussy when laid down. Do you have relatives who feel it is their duty to hold your baby all day? Are you just getting back from a long trip? evaluate the possible sources of the problem and make the appropriate changes, knowing it might take two to three days to get your baby back on track. Do what you must to protect his naptimes.

2. Our child is now standing in his crib but does not know how to get back down and begins to cry. What should we do?

Standing in the crib is only half of a newly-acquired skill. The other half is learning how to get back down after standing. You can aid the process by taking a few minutes after each nap to show him how to sit down. Take his hands firmly and guide them down the crib slats, helping him sit. Over time, he will get used to the sensation of letting himself down. If you go in every time to help him sit down, you will delay the learning process. Try looking at things from your baby's point of view: why bother learning to sit if Mom always comes to the rescue?

3. Our child keeps losing his pacifier at night and begins to cry. What should we do?

It is probably time to wean him from the pacifier to prevent both Baby and parents from becoming sleep-deprived.

4. Our baby throws off his covers at night, gets cold, and then begins to cry. What do we do?

Children move around in their sleep, making it difficult to stay covered. As parents, you have three preventive options: dressing your child warmly at night, turning up your central heating or purchasing a safe room heater. Be careful not to place your baby too close to a heater, because it is a greater health threat to become overheated than to be cold. Heaters also tend to dry the air, potentially causing respiratory problems in babies.

5. My husband and I will be traveling for the next couple of weeks. How do we maintain our baby's routine, especially when we move through different time zones?

Before leaving, give your baby opportunities to sleep in other places besides his crib. This can be done by using his playpen for some naps or nighttime sleep. For a few nights, put his playpen in the living room, family room or your bedroom, draping two sides with a couple of blankets. The blankets reduce potential distractions by closing in your child's sleep environment. If you can, take the playpen and the same blankets on your trip; if not, then borrow some blankets and a playpen when you arrive.

If your trip is within two time zones, time adjustments will be fairly automatic. When flying through three to four time zones, make adjustments to your baby's routine once you arrive. The type of adjustment depends on whether you are traveling east to west or west to east. With the first, you have an extended day; with the second, you have an early night. If you have an extended day, add another feeding and possibly a catnap. If you go west to east, split the bedtime difference in half between the old and new time zones. If your baby's West coast bedtime is 7:00 p.m., the east coast equivalent is 10:00 p.m. splitting the difference between the two zones makes your baby's first east coast bedtime at 8:30 p.m. Over the next few days, work his bedtime up to 10:00 p.m., adjusting his daytime routine as needed.

6. My seven-month-old still fusses for 5 to 10 minutes at each nap. Will he ever outgrow it, or am I doing something wrong?

Yes, your baby will outgrow it. Some babies tend to fuss more than others before settling into their naps. Science cannot offer a complete explanation as to why some babies have a greater predisposition toward fussiness and seem to need a good cry once a day. As long as your baby is not hungry, sick or in pain, but is taking good naps, that short period of fussing will eventually be a thing of the past.

7. My baby is sleeping 13 hours at night. Is this a problem?

Yes, it is. The *cause* is usually (but not always) poor or nonexistent daytime naps. Your baby is sleeping longer at night from fatigue realized during the day. Work on getting your baby's naps well established. As you do, his nighttime sleep will fall into a normal range. The *effect* of extended nighttime sleep is the negative impact it has on a nursing mother's milk production. When you do the math, you will quickly realize that the remaining 11 hours in the day are not enough time to replenish or maintain adequate nutrition through breastfeeding. If the extended sleep problem persists, contact your pediatrician.

Summary

As your baby grows into the pretoddler stage, the amount of sleep needed in a 24-hour period will gradually decline, although the quality of sleep will remain. This decline comes during the daytime, as your baby's nap schedule transitions from three naps to two, and then from two naps to one. Any problems you encounter with your baby's sleep will be minor compared to the giant strides made in stabilizing his sleep schedule.

Chapter Ten

Topic Pool

While most basic questions relating to a pretoddler's feeding, waketime and naptime transitions were addressed in earlier chapters, there are always a few secondary, independent babyhood topics in need of comment or clarification. We arranged the topics below in alphabetical order for easy reference. The list includes:

Achievement Levels
Baby equipment
Baby Proofing and Boundaries
Baby Teeth and Dental care
Brain Enhancement Videos
Church nurseries and Babysitters
Immunizations
Microwave and the Bottle
Mozart effect and Classical Music

ACHIEVEMENT LEVELS

Much has been written about what a baby is supposed to be doing physically and developmentally during the first year, such as shaking a rattle, reaching for bright objects, saying "Dada," crawling and finally, walking. There are three facts to consider when measuring your child against the "norm" table of achievement:

1. A daily routine will enhance a baby's ability to learn and process information. Repetition and predictability are key elements to learning, so establishing a consistent routine is one of the most helpful things parents can do to help their babies achieve.

2. Babies differ in age when they master many of the early skills. If your sister's nine-month-old is starting to pull himself onto a chair, and your nine-month-old is still happily crawling, there is no cause for alarm. By the time they both go to school, they both will be walking, talking, feeding themselves and using the bathroom on their own!

3. Along with your baby's physical development comes corresponding mental acumen. Be careful not to focus so much on your baby's physical accomplishments that you

let other aspects of training slip by. To help strike the right balance, you might consider reviewing the information contained in chapter One under the subheading, "Factors of Growth."

BABY EQUIPMENT

Next to a playpen and stroller, the most popular pieces of baby equipment include the Bumbo seat, infant swing, Johnny Jumper, baby walker and activity center.

The Bumbo Seat®

Providing your baby opportunities for investigating and manipulating objects is essential for brain development. Laying your baby on a blanket is one way and the Bumbo seat provides another. The Bumbo seat is actually a trademarked name and a product from south Africa. As is the case in the world of children's accessories, a number of similar seats are now being marketed from a variety of manufacturers.

The Bumbo seat style provides the right support for babies who are just starting the transition from lying on their tummies to sitting up on their own. In the sitting position, Baby can more easily manipulate or investigate a toy, which encourages longer attention spans, leading to longer sustained waketimes. The longer the waketime the more he learns.

Although marketed for ages 3 to 14 months, Bumbo-type seats offer no significant benefit once a baby is sitting up by himself, which usually occurs between six and nine months of age. The Bumbo seat does come with a few common sense warnings, such as never placing the seat on any elevated object, including a chair, bench or table. Tipping is possible, if your child move his weight off-center by stretching his back. For extra caution, when the seat is on the floor, Mom can surround Baby with pillows or a thick blanket.

The Infant Swing

A swing helps keep a baby peacefully occupied so Mom or Dad can get things done. Although the swing is no substitute for human contact—and certainly not a substitute for cuddling—it can, however, help soothe a fussy baby when nothing else works.

Infant swings have come a long way since we purchased our first one over 40 years ago. Today, just about every conceivable option is available, including swings that play music as they move. The two most common features are multiple speeds, when the swing is in motion, and a reclining option. Fussy babies tend to settle down better with the swinging motion set at a stronger setting and speed while a slower speed is more conducive for relaxed, non-fussy times. The reclining option works well if you use the swing after a feeding since it helps take pressure off Baby's full tummy.

Stay mindful of this simple truth: Your baby does not care about the various accessories that can attach to his swing, so you shouldn't either. Manufacturers tend to think in terms of what parents will buy more than what babies actually need. However, there are a few cautions to consider when using an infant swing that come with or without the fancy accessories.

First, the American Academy of Pediatrics recommends holding off the introduction of the infant swing *until a baby is able to sit up on his own*. However, most grandmothers will tell you that once a baby has good head and upper-back control, a mother can introduce the swing in the reclining position. Make sure the baby is propped well and fully secured, so he cannot slip out.

Second, swings should not be used for extended periods of time or out of Mom or Dad's visual range. When using the swing while accomplishing a task, like preparing dinner, make sure your baby can see you and that you are interacting with him. Tell him what you are doing and ask him questions, keeping him engaged. Talking to your baby promotes learning because your voice is entertaining and soothing.

Third, whether you purchase a new swing or borrow one, make sure it is assembled well, has a wide base and a low center of gravity. While tipping over is rare, it can happen if your baby leans too far over in one direction, is too big for the swing, or if the swing is not centered correctly. Make sure there is a sturdy lap belt or shoulder harness and always use them.

Finally, there will be times when your baby will fall asleep in the swing but be careful not to let it become a "sleep prop." When it is time for your baby to sleep, put him in his crib. That is not to say you cannot use the swing to help your baby fall asleep when he is teething or over-stimulated and cannot settle himself, but those are times of exception not the norm.

Johnny Jump Up®

The jumper (which goes by a variety of names including Jolly Jumper and Johnny Jump up) facilitates gross motor skills, including balance and coordination, and increases circulation. Attached securely to a door or archway, the jumper provides babies plenty of exercise and entertainment. Like the swing however, set reasonable time limits and never leave your baby untended.

The Baby Walker

The health risks associated with mobile baby walkers far outweigh any potential benefits they may offer. Since walkers are responsible for sending more than 14,000 babies to the hospital each year, the AAP has called for a ban on the sale of this piece of baby equipment. If you choose to use a walker, please be extremely careful, and under no circumstances, let your baby out of your sight. Keep the walker away from stairs, wires and any electric cords on the floor. Added to that list are any items with moving parts, such as electric fans used in the summer months or space heaters during winter.

The Activity Center

There are a variety of exercisers for babies that serve as interactive learning centers by making fun sounds, playing music and showing bright lights. A stationary activity center, such as an Exersaucer® is a better alternative for your baby than the walker mentioned above. (Exersaucer is one of many brand names). The activity center is shaped like a walker, but Baby cannot propel himself because there are no wheels. Placed inside the activity center, your baby can sit or stand and turn while examining, touching and discovering an assortment of bells, rattles and bright gadgets designed to entertain.

BABY-PROOFING OR HOME-PROOFING?

Once your baby begins to crawl, stand and move about, it will be necessary to establish those areas and items that are off limits to his exploring hands. Will your baby understand the *why* behind your instruction? No, but at this point in his development he does possess the capacity to understand what "no" or "Do not touch" mean.

There is a difference between "baby-proofing and "home proofing." To "baby-proof" your home means that you will physically rearrange your living area, so your child is never placed in a situation where you would have to limit his freedom of exploration or confront him with the feared words, "no, do not touch." Baby-proofing advocates believe any restrictions or verbal limitations initiated by the parents towards a child, regardless of the context of such limitations, will negatively impact the child's ability to learn in the future. Of course, this is all conjecture since there are no studies that lend support to this idea.

In contrast, "Home-proofing" your child means setting appropriate limitations on your pretoddler's mobility, and gradually introducing freedoms when his safety is no longer the primary concern. The practice of "home-proofing" has a moral dimension as well. As your child learns to respect the items in your living room, he carries the same self-control to your neighbor's living room and then, into society at large.

Practical Training about Boundaries

Every child under age two lives in the world of *me, myself* and *I.* Setting boundaries begins to move his restricted view of the world from self to others, because tangible property is involved. Since this is the world he will live in for the rest of his life, you want to *begin as you mean to go*.

Children nearing their first birthday have a growing awareness of boundaries. If he is faced with the temptation to play with Dad's fishing magazines on the coffee table or redirect his little hands, redirecting can win out. How can a parent move their pretoddler to this point? Instead of rearranging your home (baby-proofing), teach your pretoddler which objects are free to touch and which objects are off limits. It is in a child's nature to oppose any restrictions, but those occasions are minimized if the following reasonable steps are followed:

1. Be consistent: If an item is off limits today, it needs to be off limits tomorrow. Try not to provide freedoms that you have to take away at a future date.

2. Take necessary precautions: If you have a valuable, breakable or dangerous item within your pretoddler's reach, move it to a safe place. Install safety latches on lower cabinets, and secure any bookcases to the wall; and place "knick-knacks" and other fragile items out of reach. It is important

that parents take every precaution to make their child's environment safe. Making your home safe for a young child is not the same thing as *baby-proofing* your home.

3. Limit their play areas: If your son or daughter develops a fondness for the toilet seat in the bathroom, shut the door and keep it closed. Limiting the play area spares you and your active pretoddler unnecessary frustration.

BABY TEETH AND DENTAL CARE

Teething begins when a tooth begins to break through the gum. Teething is not a disease, but a part of the normal growth process. Most babies begin cutting their first tooth around six months of age, but it can happen anytime between four to eight months. Once the first tooth emerges, the other teeth follow at a predictable rate. The two lower-middle teeth come in first, followed by the two upper-middle teeth. Around 12 months, the two upper incisors break through, followed by the lower incisors. The first molars typically appear around 13 months of age.

For some babies, cutting a tooth might happen overnight without any sensation of pain. However, most babies do experience some discomfort because of soreness and swelling in the gums before a tooth breaks through. You might notice your baby biting a toy. This action actually helps to relieve the pressure in his gums. Most babies will drool more than normal, be slightly more irritable, or feed less vigorously. These symptoms usually appear three to five days before the tooth shows, and disappear as soon as the tooth breaks the skin.

Ideally, your baby should see a dentist right after his first tooth comes in, or at the very least, by his first birthday. This is very important because early evaluation and education are the keys to preventing dental disease. Your dentist will determine your child's risk for decay and show you how to clean his teeth effectively and safely. Visiting the dentist at an early age will also help him become comfortable in a dental office.

Severe early-childhood tooth decay is devastating. In some cases, the disease can be so advanced that by the time the child is evaluated, he will require general anesthesia to safely complete the needed treatments. Prevention is the way to go!

Teeth Cleaning and Preventing Decay

Begin cleaning your baby's teeth when the first tooth appears. Using a wet washcloth, gently rubbing against the tooth is all that is needed. While there are some baby-size toothbrushes on the market, they are not necessary; neither is toothpaste at this early age. Clean your baby's teeth at least twice a day with special attention at night just before bedtime.

Never let your baby go to bed with a bottle or sippy cup that has anything other than water. The American Academy of Pediatric Dentists recommends that you offer juice only after your baby's first birthday, only during waketimes, and only in a cup. Infants and toddlers who suffer from tooth decay are more likely to have similar problems when they get their permanent teeth. Start good habits early, like cleaning teeth twice daily, limiting juice and sugary snacks, and regularly visiting the dentist. Start good habits for life long health.

BRAIN-ENHANCEMENT VIDEOS

Some parents think they can stuff knowledge into their infant's developing brain like a deli-master stuffs a sausage! Plopping your infant in front of a television set for his daily regime of "brain-stimulating videos" or attempting to teach your eight-month-old math or Swahili will not create the world's next Einstein. Far from it! The mere quantity of facts is meaningless without establishing a healthy infrastructure for learning that brings meaning to those facts.

The outcry against educational videos targeting the parents of infants has led to complaints filed with the branch of the Federal Trade commission (FTC) responsible for dealing with false advertisement (May 11, 2006). Research strongly suggests that television viewing for babies works against cognitive development, regular sleep patterns, time spent interacting with parents, and being engaged in creative play. Television viewing can also be habit-forming and, for older children, is linked to childhood obesity and poor school performance.

Published studies in the August 8, 2007, edition of the *Journal of Pediatrics* confirm that for every hour an infant spends watching baby videos, there is a corresponding drop in language development. Children who watched videos as babies scored lower on standardized vocabulary tests than children who did not watch videos at all. The American Academy of Pediatrics advises that children under the age of two watch no television or other screen entertainment, including computer images.

There is little debate among educational clinicians that a child's ability to learn is tied to how the brain organizes information and items that stimulate thoughts, ideas and responses. When you structure learning opportunities into your child's day, you aid the learning process; but you will impede it if you overload your baby's senses with random images and facts. Your pretoddler's brain is not set up for passive, single-direction learning that comes from multicolored video animations, regardless of how a product is marketed or what it promises. Colorful, fast-moving, and bouncing images that fill a screen do not facilitate brain organization; they actually work against it.

All children, especially infants, need two-way human interaction that comes from Mom and Dad. Your baby needs to hear your voice, participate in conversations and have songs directed at him while cuddling, nursing or playing. Your baby's brain interacts far more with the real thing – Mom or Dad – than with a TV screen. Live stimulation facilitates better brain organization because more senses are stimulated: sight, sound, smell and touch, as well as the warm, loving feeling associated with the protective environment of Mom and Dad's arms.

Talk, talk, talk to your baby while feeding, playing, dressing, walking or riding in the car. Use regular speech, not baby talk. Read to your baby everyday. Stimulate your pretoddler's memory skills through infant games like "peek-a-boo" and "pat-a-cake." Get siblings and Grandma and Grandpa involved. You can help your baby develop eye-hand coordination by providing age-appropriate toys, such as blocks or anything else safe that he can manipulate with his hands. Even a few clean pot holders will do the trick.

The human factor cannot be replaced or outsourced. Educational videos for infants are a contradiction in terms. Screen images are always moving, making it difficult for your baby to process the information in an orderly way. Further, there is no pre-existing understanding to tie those images to anything. It is just a fact of development that the more the responsive side of your child's brain is left unattended during video input, the less organized the brain becomes, and the greater the potential for learning disorders, including deficiencies in focusing and concentrating.

CHURCH NURSERIES AND BABYSITTERS

Nursery and day-care workers usually have their hands full with a number of children. Because of that fact, they cannot keep track of the different routines of each child in their care. We suggest parents leave a snack and a bottle of water, formula or breastmilk; then give the attendant the freedom to do what she thinks is best for your baby in those moments when your baby has a need that falls outside of his normal routine.

When you have a well-established routine, a few hours in a nursery setting will not throw your child off. You can make the appropriate adjustments when you and Baby get home. That is the beauty of having an established schedule. It allows for flexibility when most needed, but provides for the smoothest operation of your average day.

The babysitter who provides a service in your home (or in her own home with only a few other babies) can follow your routine much easier than a nursery or day-care worker who must care for 10 other babies. If that is the case with your baby, write out your baby's schedule, establish clear expectations, and you are on your way to a good working relationship that benefits everyone involved.

IMMUNIZATIONS

The ability to protect our children from the tragedies of polio and other deadly diseases is one of the great blessings of our day. Medical research has provided us with effective immunizations that build up antibodies to fight off invading diseases, but those vaccines are useless to you if your child never receives them. Parents are responsible to see that their children are fully protected. The eight common vaccinations offered are against polio, diphtheria, pertussis (whooping cough), tetanus, rubella (German measles), mumps, measles, hepatitis and Haemophilus influenza, type B (HiB). Most pediatricians start routine immunizations within the first two months after a baby is born.

Continue checking with your pediatrician for a current timetable of vaccinations, because immunization schedules change frequently as better vaccines and updated research becomes available. Make sure your child is receiving his on schedule. If you have concerns or questions about any vaccine, speak with your pediatrician. He or she will be a more reliable source of information than Internet chat rooms and articles on the pro's and con's of vaccinations.

MICROWAVE AND THE BOTTLE

For babies receiving formula, Mom or Dad will naturally want to take advantage of the microwave to heat a bottle of formula. Loosen the top of the bottle to allow for heat expansion so it does not literally explode. Be aware that microwaves heat food unevenly, creating hot spots, so be sure to shake the bottle well after heating and squirt a dab of milk on your wrist to test for warmth.

Because excessive heat can destroy the nutrient quality of expressed breastmilk, we recommend that you avoid using the microwave to thaw or heat it. Instead, place the bottle of expressed breastmilk in a bowl or small pan of warm water.

Whether your baby is getting breastmilk or formula, most will take a bottle at one time or another. It is important to keep the bottles and nipples clean and sterilized. This is safest with a bottle sterilizer designed to work in your microwave. They are available at major stores that sell baby items and come in various models and price ranges. A dishwasher can do the job with cages that hold the nipples and other small items, but only if you tend to wipe your dishes and utensils visibly clean before loading them (that is, you do not treat your dishwasher like a garbage disposal). It helps to shake down the bottles and other items that retain water when the rinse cycle stops so they dry properly during your dishwasher's drying phase.

MOZART EFFECT AND CLASSICAL MUSIC

Filling the airways of your home with classical music as a way of providing an educational edge to infants and toddlers is an growing topic of interest. What is called the "Mozart effect" was based on a study done in 1993 that suggested listening to Mozart can increase spatial reasoning, which aids logic. While the research was done on college students and not with babies, the findings are worth some consideration.

Music is a unique language with the ability to bypass a listener's mind and speak directly to the heart. Classical music is very orderly in its construction, and order promotes a peaceful spirit. That is particularly true for music composed by Bach and Mozart. Mankind has the ability to listen to music on two levels. On the surface, we hear a song and its melody. Below the surface, just above the subconscious level, we hear the logic of the melody, although we rarely pay attention to this. It is theorized that when young children are exposed to classical music, it strengthens the logic center of the brain, so areas dependent on logic, such as mathematics and complex reasoning, are reinforced.

While there is some limited evidence supporting this conclusion, science cannot tell us to what extent babies actually relate to expressions of logic through the medium of music. We do know babies relate to the logic found in predictability that is connected to orderliness and routine; so the possibility that logical patterns are being reinforced through this type of music has at least some theoretical plausibility.

PLAYPEN ADVANTAGES

In previous chapters, we introduced the playpen and Playpen Time. This section expands that conversation by looking at the many advantages of the playpen.

1. *It provides a safe environment*. A playpen is a safe place to put your baby when your attention must be elsewhere. Having the baby in a playpen enables Mom to take a shower, unload groceries from the car, care for other children, and do a host of other activities—all while knowing her baby is safe.

2. *It doubles as a portable bed*. The playpen can serve as a portable bed, especially useful when visiting another family's home. The playpen gives your baby a clean, familiar place to sleep.

3. *It offers a structured learning center*. The playpen encourages a love for learning because babies are in a place where their little world is uninterrupted. There are no distractions, and it is the right-size venue for helping babies focus and concentrate as they play. Playpen Time helps a child develop the ability to concentrate on an object or activity at hand. Observe how a child picks up a toy, manipulates it with his hands, examines it carefully, shakes it or removes a part, examines it and then tests his skills by repeating the process again. The joy of discovering how something works becomes the motivation that perpetuates a longer attention span and deeper levels of concentration. These are academic attributes required for higher learning, and they are greatly encouraged during playpen time.

When routine and structured-learning times are absent in a baby's day, the repertoire of skills he might otherwise attain is delayed or compromised. The playpen is all about creating the right learning environment.

4. <u>*It promotes orderliness.*</u> The first step to developing orderliness is teaching your child to participate with cleanup. The smaller the area to clean up, the easier the job will be. Start by placing a few books in one corner of the playpen, a bucket of small toys in another or stacking items in a neat pile. A simple statement like, "Let's put the toys in the basket," aids the process. The object is to leave the playpen neat for the next play-time with your child participating in the process. This simple exercise encourages orderliness and is carried forward as your child learns to keep his room tidy.

When to Use the Playpen

Schedule your Playpen Times at approximately the same time each day when your baby is freshest and most alert—not before naptime. Put one or two interesting toys within Baby's reach or put the toys in a small basket, and place the basket in the playpen. Always stay mindful of keeping the toys age-appropriate. The child who finds a shiny blue rattle fascinating at five months will ignore it at ten months. Local libraries carry books that describe the types of toys or activities your baby is likely to be interested in at each stage of development. Your pediatrician's office can also help you on that subject.

One important aspect of selecting appropriate toys is acknowledging what are not toys: tools, markers, cell phones, car keys and anything else that is private and personal property. Mom's earrings, billfold and lipstick in her purse—the purse itself, for that matter—are not toys. Neither is Dad's pocket pen, reading glasses or watch. Think about it: If you amuse your baby with general and personal items now, will those same play items be off limits in a few months? If they will not be appropriate toys then, should they be allowed now? Babies have a lot more sense than we give them credit for.

If you have twins, alternate their times in the playpen. Put one in the playpen in the morning, the other in the afternoon. Occasionally, try putting them both in at the same time. If your home allows for it, vary the location of the playpen from time to time. For example, during the week you might put it in the living room. Then on the weekend, place it near the sliding-glass door overlooking the backyard where older siblings are playing. In warm weather, take the playpen outside.

Position the playpen so that you can easily check on your baby without your baby seeing you. It detracts from the purpose of self-directed playtime if the child can see Mom or Dad. Essentially forcing a child to choose between actively learning to occupy himself or passively watching Mom in the next room is not fair to him. If you live in a small apartment, be creative. For example, you might use a portable room divider to section off part of the living room or bedroom.

The time your baby spends in the playpen will vary with age. During the first few months, your baby may have 10 to 20 minutes, twice a day in the playpen. By the time your baby can sit by himself, you can extend playpen time to 15 to 30 minutes, twice a day. Once your baby starts to crawl, increase the time to 30 to 45 minutes at least once a day. Between 15 and 20 months, your child can play up to one hour either in the playpen or possibly in his room. These are suggested guidelines, of course. Some days your child will play longer, other days for shorter periods.

Do not overuse the playpen by leaving your baby in it for extended and unplanned periods during the day. Playpen Time should be a planned activity, not an all-day event. As a word of encouragement, children of all ages have a love/hate relationship with boundaries. They hate boundaries simply because they are there, yet they love them because of the security they provide. If your child does not appear to like the playpen at first, stay with it for at least five minutes until he accepts it. Rest assured, the playpen will become a fun place for your baby.

Keeping the Timer Handy

The use of a timer is very beneficial when first starting playpen training. Whether your child adapts with perfect ease or cries in protest, you want him to learn Playpen Time is over when the timer goes off, not when he cries. If you do not use a timer, your baby may be tempted to cry without ceasing, thinking his crying is what brings Mom or Dad to the rescue rather than Playpen Time just happened to be done.

Starting Late

How should you introduce the playpen if it has not been part of your baby's day up to now? Start with short periods of time—maybe 5 to 10 minutes a day. Over the next two to three weeks, work up to 20 minutes, then 30 minutes. After a month, consider extending the time to 45 minutes. Playpen Time will eventually become a fun activity for your pretoddler.

SLEEP AND LEARNING

Let's start with adult reality: last night was a rough one. The dog was barking, and the electricity went out from a severe thunderstorm, causing the alarm clock by your bed to fry when the power came on again. Throughout the ordeal, you never got out of bed. You do not recall being awake, although you figured out something had happened when your alarm did not go off. Now you are cranky, edgy and just not nice to be around. Simply put, you got a lousy night's sleep, and every raw nerve in your body is ready to let everyone you meet know this. Did you ever stop to think your children might go through experiences like this?

When it comes to pretoddlers, parents tend to think in terms of these two things only: either their child is asleep or awake. Actually, there are blending scales of sleep and wakefulness. Sleep ranges from a completely relaxed state to active sleep; wakefulness ranges from groggy to completely alert. Optimal wakefulness is tied to optimal sleep and optimal development to optimal wakefulness. We cannot overemphasize that point. Pretoddlers and preschoolers who suffer from a lack of healthy naps and nighttime sleep experience "passive chronic fatigue."

Too little sleep is devastating to your child's alertness. It increases his inattentiveness while decreasing his ability to focus and concentrate. He will be easily distracted and often physically hyperactive. He will also be more demanding and unable to interact within a learning environment for sustained periods of time.

In contrast, children who have established healthy sleep habits are optimally awake and alert, ready to interact with their environment. Having now observed a generation of these children, we see common threads when they reach school age. In classroom settings, these children are more self-assured, happier, less demanding, more sociable, creative and motivated. They have longer attention spans and become faster learners because they are more adaptable. Mediocrity among these children is rare, and excellence is common.

In *Babywise*, we spoke of a child's ability to learn. We noted that while parents cannot alter a child's intelligence quotient (IQ), they can maximize or limit it. One way is through sleep, as first noted in a 1925 study conducted by Dr. Lewis M. Terman. His insights and conclusions relating to factors influencing IQ stand unchallenged to this day. He looked at over 2,000 children with superior intelligence and found one common factor: all of them had experienced consistent healthy nighttime sleep. Good sleep habits are not a child's choice, but a parent's decision and commitment.

THE WALKING MILESTONE

A pretoddler's mobility begins by creeping, then crawling, standing, moving from object to object, and then, one day it happens: he takes his first steps! His world changes and so does Mom and Dad's. Walking is a developmental milestone that marks a new era of independence. Now his little feet can take him where his mind desires. If he is on the go, you should not be far behind.

Walking also ushers in a new era of parental supervision because it increases a child's contacts. Mobility opens doors of opportunity and new areas of interest, exploration and adventure, which require constant parental supervision. Now your baby is also able to walk to mischief and trouble. As a crawler, you knew his range of exploration; as a walker, you must stay more attentive to where he is. Keep your eye on him because his ability and resolve to get from here to there far outweigh his judgment for caution and safety. Now, Mom will need sleep like never before!

During the one-year span between 12 and 24 months, the walking, talking, exploring pretoddler multiplies the demands of his mother's time, energy and patience more than any other period of his life. It is also a time when clashes of the will abound, for the pretoddler is testing not only his legs, but also trying new experiences with his hands. His mind is catching up with his legs, so asserting himself accompanies his mobility. If left to himself, unhindered by moral and safety concerns, this little person could empty a bookshelf in minutes, connect with Hong Kong on Dad's cell phone, drink from the birdbath, splash in the toilet, drain the last sips of a beverage left on the coffee table, flee the kitchen with a table knife, and take a nap in the doghouse—all for starters!

The emotional and physical energy needed to supervise an energy-packed tot will drain the most physically fit mom. If your child happens to be a boy, add 50 percent more energy. Never so beautiful does this child look to his weary mom as when he closes his eyes in sleep. Some babies begin walking at nine months while others wait until 18 months. Walking does not take away from the advantages gained by your baby's routine, but it does challenge everything within the routine. Rest assured that the feeding, waketime and naptime strategies you are learning in *Babywise II* will help you manage your soon-to-be mobile child.

BOOK SUMMARY

There is no greater fulfillment a parent can receive than the upturned face of a child, eyes speaking wonders from discovering a brand new world with Mom and Dad. While there is work to be done in the remaining pretoddler days, the foundations you have laid during the 5 to 12-month phase will be rock solid for building on the next phase of growth and development when parenting your 12 to 18-month-old. When you and your baby arrive at the point in time, everything will change again, as his awareness of the meaning of life begins to accelerate, and your strategies for care grow more complex.

Infancy will soon be a thing of the past and toddlerhood is just around the corner. While change may usher in a new sense of urgency for you, one constant to stay reminded of is the need to "*begin as you mean to go*" and stay on that track! Enjoy the remainder of the *Babywise II* phase!

Appendix A

Child Language Development

Anyone attempting to learn a new language will tell you that it can be a very difficult task, and it can take years to achieve a level of fluency. Babies are equipped with a phenomenal ability to achieve total fluency in about three years, with very little practice and almost no conscious thought required. Parents are the models God has provided for a child's development, and the area of language development is no different from the many others discussed in this guide.

In your infant's world, there are only sounds, no words. The more you talk to your baby the stronger the formation of a dedicated connection in the brain's auditory cortex. The more words your baby hears *from you*, the faster he develops his language skills. Here are some ideas to help your child in his language skills.

1. It is not necessary to use "baby talk." It is very tempting to reduce what you are saying to what you think the baby understands, such as "Ryan, no touch, that bad." children are wonderful decoders. If you say, "Ryan, don't touch that, it's bad," he will (even at the young age of six months) understand the tone of voice, the facial expression, and any gestures you might use. By 12–14 months, he will understand enough of the words and intonations to figure out exactly what you are telling him. Children are wonderful imitators, too. Why not give them a chance to learn the correct sentence structure by speaking it yourself?

2. Talk about anything and everything! This gives your child a chance to pair words with concepts. Even though he will not understand all the words at first, what a great exposure to the world you are giving him! When you go to the grocery store, talk about what you are getting, where you are going next, things you see in the aisles. A pretoddler certainly does not understand everything, but you are laying a broad foundation for the future.

3. Read, read, read! Reading books to your child is a wonderful way to expose him to words and concepts. (We recommend Jim Trelease's *Read-Aloud Handbook*, Penguin Books: n.Y., n.Y.) which helps children become avid readers.

4. Once your child starts speaking, expand on what he says. For example, you are giving your son a bath, and he says,

"Boat down." You could respond by saying, "Yes, the boat went down." This not only recognizes what your child has said, but also gives him the correct form of a full sentence. Cute as it may be, you really do not want your child to start kindergarten using baby sentences!

5. Above all, relax! With few exceptions, children learn language in spite of anything parents do or think they have done to inhibit it!

CHILD LANGUAGE DEVELOPMENT

The following is a general outline of the stages of child language development. Each child develops at his own rate, and the ages given are approximate.

Birth to 3 months: A familiar, friendly voice comforts him. He smiles at Mom or another familiar person. He has different cries for hunger, dirty diaper, and fatigue. He coos and goos.

2 to 4 months: He pays attention to the person speaking to him, responds to an angry tone of voice by crying, and turns toward a source of sound. He laughs out loud and begins to babble making sounds like "bababa."

4 to 6 months: He begins to respond to his environment and begins to understand inflection and intensity of utterances. He strings several different sounds together "badaba-daba," and he blows raspberries.

6 to 9 months: He listens with greater attention to others' utterances, understands words such as "no," "bye-bye," and his name. He begins to echo sounds and actions that others make.

9 to 12 months: He begins following simple directions ("Do not touch," "come here!") and shakes his head yes and no. The long-awaited first word appears and he begins to use "jargon" (strings of sounds paired with intonations to sound like questions, statements, or demands).

12 to 18 months: He recognizes familiar objects and people and identifies body parts. He adds more and more words and begins to put short sentences together.

18 to 24 months: He identifies more and more objects when requested to do so and listens to simple stories.

The ages listed above are only a guide and indicate when most children exhibit the language skill listed. Do not worry if your child is a month or two late at attaining any given level, for children mature at different rates. If your child is not responding to you by the age of one year, or not speaking at all by the age of two years, you should seek referrals to the appropriate professionals from your child's doctor.

Finally, just as a reminder—early video watching for children under the age of two will have a negative effect on speech development. This is one reason the American Academy of Pediatrics does not endorse screen images for infants. Your baby's brain has circuits in the auditory cortex representing sounds that form words. They become hard-wired by the age of one year. Research strongly suggest the more words a child hears by the age of two years, the larger his vocabulary. However, the method by which words are transferred is as important as the words themselves. During these early ages, nothing beats the human factor and the two-way communication that comes from Mom and Dad's voice. This is something videos cannot do!

Appendix B

What Makes Your Baby a Person

Nature has a keen way of tutoring parents. Observe the gardener with his plants. He does not create the bloom or the petal, or the stem that produces the petal. He cannot grow the plant or make it more beautiful. He is neither its creator nor its architect. The power of life and beauty lies within the plant itself. The gardener, however, knows the environment. He knows the right amount of sunshine and moisture required for the unfolding of every blossom. He knows the time of pruning, training, and fertilizing that is necessary to bring the plant to a beautiful bloom. Yet the gardener is neither the life of the plant nor the source, but he is the nurturer of the life placed before him.

Picture your baby's life unfolding like a beautiful bloom. You, the parent, serve as the bloom's keeper. No other influence can affect the life of your child quite like you—a loving, caring parent. You are more than a nurturer of nature; you are the guardian. You matter greatly in the life formation of your child. This leads us to observe the real work of parents as loving mentors.

We know that your emerging pretoddler has his own peculiar way. He will think in the here and now, with no tomorrow in sight. He is not easily moved to self-restraint, nor does he seek to secure some future blessings. "A penny saved is a penny earned" is quite beyond his grasp and interest. And all his nursery peers would agree that crying over spilled milk is essential if you are really thirsty—you will get more milk faster that way!

As your pretoddler transitions into the early stages of toddlerhood, he will first be concerned with the concrete, not the abstract. Moral qualities such as justice, mercy, and truth are quite beyond his reach, but he does understand these qualities when expressed toward him. His actions and developing speech reflect his self-oriented desires rather than socialized values that will change in a few years.

Clearly the adult life, while distinct from childhood and adolescence, is wholly built upon the foundation of early training parents put into their children. It is important to see that a child is adequately prepared from the beginning for a safe arrival in the many stations of life, starting with understanding all the components that make up the little soon-to-be crawling person emerging under your roof.

What goes into making your baby a person? Apart from the spiritual elements reflecting the creator's thumbprint on your baby's soul, there are a variety of biological influences, including things you cannot control (i.e. nature, heredity, temperament, and predispositions), and those influences shaped by your beliefs, including nurture, environment, education, values, and goals.

There is also the natural order of growth and development of children bringing new and changing variables into play. As the baby's body grows, so grows his mind, and so grows his interplay with the rest of humanity. These factors combined make up the human quality of our being.

To prepare your thinking for what awaits you just around the developmental corner, consider the influence of *heredity, environment* and the factors shaping your child's *personality*.

Your Baby's Life is Controlled by HEP

Little Joey swings a stick, and suddenly he is slated for college All-stars 20 years down the road. Abby twists a silk scarf around her neck, and she is destined to be a fashion designer following her momma's footsteps. Far-fetched? Not exactly. We are all influenced by the forces of heredity, environment, and personality. Nineteenth century Dartmouth college professor, H. H. Horne, in his book *Idealism in Education*, links these relationships in plain words:

1. Heredity bestows capacity
2 Environment provides opportunity
3. Personality recognizes capacity and improves opportunity

Each of these forces combine together to shape all of us. The same Professor Horne is credited with saying, "A child is born in part, he is made in part, and in part he makes himself." We believe that is an accurate assessment of life. Heredity, it has been said, determines what your child can do, and environment determines what your child will do. Supervising all three aspects are the caretakers of life—Mom and Dad.

Heredity

After conception, nothing can be done to add to or subtract from our hereditary endowment. If Grandpa's left ear turns out along the back edge, just like your mother's left ear which looks amazingly like your own, guess what? Do not be surprised if one or more of your own beautiful blooms sports the telltale "Grandpa ear." Other traits, while not visible to the eye, are doled out with equal clarity. Is there a trait in your pretoddler that you do not like? Take a look at the family photos hanging in the hallway. Do you see the relative that is smirking? He is probably the one to blame.

A child inherits one-half of his genetic self from his two parents, one-fourth of his characteristics from the four grandparents, and one-eighth of his biological distinctiveness from eight great-grandparents. Heredity passes to each generation two categories of traits—fixed and fluid. Fixed genetic traits are immune to nurturing influences. Fluid tendencies, however, are greatly impacted by the nurturing process.

For example, outward distinctions such as red hair, green eyes, short arms, big ears, cute nose, and dimpled chins are fixed endowments. They are what they are, straight from the genetic cabbage patch. Have you ever wondered where that nose came from? Nothing in genetic sight among the parents? "Your baby got that from uncle Fabio on your mother's side," says Aunt Regina. A hidden surprise from the family tree.

Heredity also passes fluid endowments. These are propensities, tendencies, and capacities. Intelligence potential, aptitudes and special levels of giftedness are all fluid, meaning this side of the hereditary equation is markedly influenced by the nurturing environment. That is why heredity determines what a child can do, and the environment determines what a child will do.

We have friends endowed with the gift and talent for music. Mom and Dad each play a combination of instruments including harp, piano, trumpet, guitar, flute, trombone, French horn, and the oboe. What did their children inherit? It was not their parent's knowledge of music, but an ear, aptitude, capacity and interest in music. Natural propensities spawned in the right environment produced, in this case, multi-talented musical children. But the genetic endowment was nurtured. Without the nurturing environment, the beautiful seeds of endowment, like the frozen pods in the tundra, lie dormant until the conditions are right to bloom. Unfortunately, human environments are less predictable than seasonal ones.

What does this mean for you and your baby? If the nurturing environment is to stimulate genetic potentials and maximize those potentials, it needs three things from Mom and Dad.

First, you need awareness. In the Ezzo family line, Gary's father was a talented musician. He played a number of stringed instruments and the piano with pep. Of three sons, only one inherited the father's musical talent. Gary was not the one. In the next generation when Gary and his wife Anne Marie were raising their children, they knew there was a possibility for some musical giftedness. But possibility does not equate to certainty, and it was soon realized that no great musical genetic endowment fell on their offspring.

The point here is that of awareness. The Ezzos knew of a genetic propensity for musical ability. Because of it, they created a nurturing environment to determine if any gene slipped through the family line, and then responded to the opportunity by introducing formalized music lessons in their children's primary years.

What is in your family tree? Go back two generations, to parents and grandparents, and write up a list of endowment possibilities. Talk to relatives, great-aunts and uncles, and older cousins. Was Grandpa highly inventive? Was Mom an artisan of quilts? Was there an uncle gifted in mathematics, or a sister endowed with a massive vocabulary and a creative mind? Become aware of the genetic endowments of your recent family lineage. Maybe you'll find a squirrel in your family tree, which will finally account for Billy's need to store up every scrap of paper, every piece of ribbon, and every pebble he ever touched.

Second, you can maximize your baby's genetic potential when you parent the "whole child" rather than just a single trait. Hurray for you if your child is a budding Rembrandt, Mozart, Galileo or Edison; but can he entertain himself when playing by himself? Can he get along with other children? Can your little star kick a ball and gently spend time with baby sister? Do not err like Schroeder's mom did. Schroeder is the Peanuts character that spent his entire cartoon life hunched over a piano composing music.

While any unfavorable parent attitude can result in unhealthy outcomes, that which has the most damaging and far-reaching effect is the concept of the dream child. Parents create a genetic ideal and force the child into a very narrow category of interest. As a result, the emotional pressure to attain dream-child status, mixed with the lack of normal childhood experiences, hinders genetic potential, if not wounding it.

Third, no wonderful gift of hereditary endowment can be matured if not surrounded by the basic disciplines of life. Writing the latest, greatest American novel will be impossible if your would-be author never develops the focus needed for reading. Piano practice becomes a battle if your child never learned to sit and concentrate. Yes, there is that playpen thing again. Sitting, focusing, concentrating.

The basic point here is this: A child cannot learn until he is ready to learn, nor can he achieve until his biological clock says it is time. He cannot master any skill without the accompanying resources of self-control and self-governance. This means that regardless of what giftedness or talent your child possesses, or what wonderful genetic endowment he may have inherited, it needs to be nurtured in the total context of childhood and childhood training. If it is not, that giftedness, while possibly discovered, will eventually reach a plateau in learning and show little improvement from that time forward. Remember the gardener analogy? Good seeds planted in poor soil will result in stunted plants. So it is with our children. That leads to some thoughts regarding the learning environment your baby is growing in.

Environment

With both heredity and environment, children are recipients. Regarding the environment, the home has dominant control. Mom and Dad provide the environment for the most impressionable years of life. The difficulty, if not the downfall of laissez-faire parenting, is not realizing how education shapes the habits of the heart, and in so doing, weds genetic propensities with right stimulation. The positive forces of heredity do not always find a healthy and nourishing environment. When good capacity is denied the right environment, the legacy is at best less than a child's full potential, and at worst, a generational disaster. What can a parent glean from this fact? One supreme thought: The beliefs that drive your parenting can and will affect generations to come. That is another way of reminding you to *begin as you mean to go.*

Personality

Energetic noah does everything big. He will march into a room, all smiles, and give Grandma a great big hug. Hopping to the room's center, he delights his eager audience with an impromptu performance. Finally, in grand finale, he drops to the floor to roll himself out the door. When Mom calls him to sit beside her, he cries, and staying true to the end, his distress and resistance is huge. Is his high-flying, crash-and-burn style a sign of a testy temperament, or are we now in the personality zone? What is the difference anyway?

Let's take a look. Few words used in contemporary theory of child development are as ambiguous as the term "personality." The term suggests a variety of meanings to different theorists. We have all heard the expression, "He's a chip off the old block," implying that personality is inherited and not subject to change. Not so on either account.

We provide a very simple definition for the sake of continuity. Personality is a composite of three variables: heredity, environment, and temperament. Temperament (inborn into human personality) speaks to the general categories of uniqueness, which greatly influence a child's perceptions and reactions. You can distinguish between a child's temperament and his personality by saying that temperament traits are inborn while personality traits are the result of nature and nurture. Heredity is what your genetic history brings to personality, environment is what the home and society add, and temperament is the child's contribution.

If that sounds confusing then take relief with this bit of news. Your child's personality is the last thing you need to worry about. That is because personality is the sum of each influence shaping the formation of our being. It is not one definite, specific attribute; rather it is the quality of the individual's total behavior. You cannot change the whole without changing the parts, and some parts cannot be changed.

For example, you cannot change your child's temperament anymore than a leopard can change its spots. You can understand it and cooperate with it, but not alter it. You cannot alter the hereditary influences on your children, but you can minimize the negative propensities, strengthen areas of weakness, encourage areas of strength, and maximize areas of giftedness.

The only area you have enormous influence over in the formation of personality is in creating the right educational environment for your baby. Education impacts personality. The learning environment fostered will make all the difference in the world for your baby and soon to be toddler.

When we speak of education, we do so in the broadest sense. This goes way beyond textbook learning. Learning and schooling are not synonymous, but both are vehicles of education. Most of your parenting will be devoted to educating your children in three vital areas of life until they achieve mastery themselves: morality, health and safety, and life skills.

Your child's personality is greatly shaped by your educational fervency. For example, in the toddler years you will begin to teach how to be kind, good, caring, patient, generous, and responsible. You will also help him form healthy habits—how to brush his teeth, take a bath, and manage his personal care.

Accenting these educational goals is more education, such as teaching the child how to think, how to make sound judgments, and how to apply logic and reason to his life.

The next major phase of your baby's development expands on all factors of learning that place you, mom and dad in the driver's seat. The good news is how far you have come already. Before you know it, the *babyhood transition* phase will soon be a thing of the past, but the foundations you laid with feeding, waketime activities and healthy sleep habits will travel with your baby into the next major milestone of life: the walking, talking, exploring mobile toddler. Happy parenting.

Subject Index

More Parenting Resources

by Gary Ezzo and Robert Bucknam

With over two million homes to their credit, trusted parenting authors Gary Ezzo and Robert Bucknam bring their collective wisdom, experience, and insights to bear on these critical phases of growth and development.

On Becoming Babywise

On Becoming Babywise gained national and international recognition for its immensely sensible approach to nurturing a newborn. The infant management plan offered by Ezzo and Bucknam successfully and naturally helps infants synchronize their feeding/waketime and nighttime sleep cycles. The results? You have a happy, healthy and contented baby who will begin sleeping through the night on average between seven and nine weeks of age.

On Becoming Babywise II

This series teaches the practical side of introducing solid foods, managing mealtimes, nap transitions, traveling with your infant, setting reasonable limits while encouraging healthy exploration and much more. You will learn how to teach your child to use sign language for basic needs, a tool proven to help stimulate cognitive growth and advance communication.

On Becoming Pretoddlerwise

The period between 12 and 18 months places a child on a one-way bridge to the future. Infancy is a thing of the past and toddlerhood is straight ahead. A baby still? Not really, but neither is he a toddler, and that is the key to understanding this phase of growth. This is a period of metamorphosis when his potential for learning seems limitless, his budding curiosity unquenchable and his energy level never seems to diminish. It is also a period of great exchange: baby food is exchanged for table food; the highchair for booster seat; finger feeding is replaced with spoon; babbling sounds will transition to speaking, the first unsteady steps are conquered by strides of confidence, and the list goes on. *On Becoming Pretoddlerwise* will help any parent acquire useful knowledge that will prepare them for what lies around the next corner – the reality of toddlerhood where change sometimes comes every day.

On Becoming Toddlerwise

The toddler years are learning fields and you need a trustworthy guide to take you through the unfolding maze of your child's developing world. *On Becoming Toddlerwise* is a toolchest of workable strategies and ideas that multiply your child's learning opportunities in a loving and nurturing way. This resource is as practical as it is informative.

On Becoming Pottywise for Toddlers
Potty training does not have to be complicated and neither should a resource that explains it. *On Becoming Pottywise for Toddlers* looks to developmental readiness cues of children as the starting point of potty training. While no promise can be made, we can tell you that many moms successfully complete their training in a day or two; some achieve it literally in hours.

On Becoming Preschoolwise
Gary Ezzo and Dr. Robert Bucknam once again bring their collective wisdom, experience, and insight to bear on this critical phase of preschool training. From teaching about the importance of play to learning how to prepare a preschooler for the first day of school, from organizing your child's week to understanding childhood fears and calming parental anxiety; sound advice and practical application await the reader.

On Becoming Childwise
Equip yourself with fifteen practical principles for training kids in the art of living happily among family and friends. Foster the safe, secure growth of your child's self-concept and worldview. *On Becoming Childwise* shows you how to raise emotionally balanced, intellectually-assertive and morally-sensible children. It is the essential guidebook for the adventurous years from toddler to grade-schooler!

On Becoming Preteenwise

The middle years, eight to twelve years of age, are perhaps the most significant attitude-forming period in the life of a child. It is during this time that the roots of moral character are established. From the foundation that is formed, healthy or not-so-healthy family relationships will be built. These are the years when patterns of behavior are firmly established—patterns that will impact your parent-child relationship for decades to come. Rightly meeting the small challenges of the middle years significantly reduces the likelihood of big challenges in the teen years.

On Becoming Teenwise

Why do teenagers rebel? Is it due to hormones, a suppressed primal desire to stake out their own domain, or a natural and predictable process of growth? To what extent do parents encourage or discourage the storm and stress of adolescence? *On Becoming Teenwise* looks at the many factors that make living with a teenager a blessing or a curse. It exposes the notions of secular myth and brings to light the proven how-to applications of building and maintaining healthy relationships with your teens. Whether you worry about your teen and dating or your teen and drugs, the principles of *On Becoming Teenwise* are appropriate and applicable for both extremes and everyone in-between. They do work!

